Supporting Trans People of Colour

of related interest

**Working with Autistic Transgender
and Non-Binary People**
Research, Practice and Experience
Edited by Marianthi Kourti
ISBN 978 1 78775 022 7
eISBN 978 1 78775 023 4

Overcoming Everyday Racism
Building Resilience and Wellbeing in the Face
of Discrimination and Microaggressions
Susan Cousins
ISBN 978 1 78592 850 5
eISBN 978 1 78592 851 2

White Privilege Unmasked
How to Be Part of the Solution
Judy Ryde
ISBN 978 1 78592 408 8
eISBN 978 1 78450 767 1

The Beginner's Guide to Being a Trans Ally
Christine Whittlesey
ISBN 978 1 78775 783 7
eISBN 978 1 78775 784 4

Supporting Trans People of Colour

How to Make Your Practice Inclusive

Sabah Choudrey

Jessica Kingsley Publishers
London and Philadelphia

First published in Great Britain in 2022 by Jessica Kingsley Publishers
An Hachette Company

1

Copyright © Sabah Choudrey 2022

The list on page 41 has been reproduced with kind permission from R. Kaur.
The list on page 70 has been reproduced with kind permission
from the Unitarian Universalist Association.
The list on page 76–77 has been reproduced with kind
permission from the BARC Collective.
The poem on page 97–98 has been reproduced with kind permission from Travis Alabanza.
The list on page 102–104 has been reproduced with kind permission from Dr Kathy Obear.
The material on page 117–118 (adapted from brown, 2017) has
been reproduced with kind permission from AK Press.

Every effort has been made to trace copyright holders and to obtain their permission
for the use of copyright material where necessary to do so. The author and the publisher
apologize for any omissions and would be grateful if notified of any acknowledgements
that should be incorporated in future reprints or editions of this book.

A CIP catalogue record for this title is available from the
British Library and the Library of Congress

ISBN 978 1 78775 059 3
eISBN 978 1 78775 060 9

Printed and bound by CPI Group (UK) Ltd, Croydon CR0 4YY

Jessica Kingsley Publishers' policy is to use papers that are natural,
renewable and recyclable products and made from wood grown in
sustainable forests. The logging and manufacturing processes are expected
to conform to the environmental regulations of the country of origin.

Jessica Kingsley Publishers
Carmelite House
50 Victoria Embankment
London EC4Y 0DZ

www.jkp.com

For Nila

Kin: I am, because we are – by blkmoodyboi

Contents

Acknowledgements

بسم الله الرحمن الرحيم

Bi-smi llāhi r-raḥmāni r-raḥīm.

I begin in the name of Allah, the most gracious, the most merciful.

Without graciousness, kindness or faith I would not be here. I want to extend and express my gratitude to everyone who has been a part of this book, to the reader for being a part of this work and to everyone who continues to protect, empower and have faith in trans people of colour.

Without the many Black and Indigenous people and people of colour who came before me, this book would not be here either; to the leaders, healers, posers, creators, pioneers, warriors, defenders and storytellers; to those whose names are unknown and whose stories are untold, their legacies always are remembered; thank you.

I am forever thankful to all the trans, non-binary and questioning youth who I've had the honour of meeting in youth clubs, in Zoom rooms, at campsites and over phone calls, texts and affirmations. They give me a hope that I don't get from anywhere else, and they show me that there are so many ways to be trans. From knocking over water bottles to pure vibes: you are valid!

I am so grateful to my incredible friends at Gendered Intelligence for giving me space to dream and imagine trans futures, for investing in my wellness and valuing my experiences, and to my wonderful friends at Colours Youth Network for making my dreams come true, centring QTIBPOC joy and slowing down together. I'm so glad our youth communities have all of you.

To Andrew James, whose phone call five or so years ago made me believe that I could do this and that this text was needed by many. To everyone at Jessica Kingsley Publishers for your patience and support throughout. To blkmoodyboi for the beautiful illustration on the inside cover and for uplifting us with their art. To all the anonymous survey respondents trusting in me and sharing their experiences in these pages. To all the people I have named throughout and shared words from. This book wouldn't be what it is without them, and our communities wouldn't be what they are without them either. Thank you.

To Yarrow Magdalena for helping me understand the world of book publishing and becoming my brand and for the most important advice: I can be cute and powerful. To Bernard and Terry Reed from GIRES, who first gave me the opportunity and power to write the resource 'Inclusivity', the first place I put these words. To Samir Jeraj for making space for trans people of colour. To Meg-John Barker, whose affirmation has been felt before we ever exchanged words. I am grateful for their encouragement through the proposal and first steps, for telling me it's okay if this takes time. To L Goddard for meeting me at the start of my trans youth-work journey and supporting me with my proposal to get here. Thank you.

Abeera, Raisa, Stephanie, Travis, thank you for inspiring me. As friends and as pioneers in their fields, they have shown me what is possible for Muslims, queers and people of colour. Hanita and Rima, my oldest friends who have known me through so much, which I am so grateful for. I couldn't have made it through this year without them – thank you for reminding me to laugh and forcing me to relax. Thank you to Raheem and Tasmia, who have been alongside me, believed in me and celebrated me; to Shiri for our friendship, writing dates and Pomodoro timers; to Martha for having continuous pride and faith in me.

I give thanks from the bottom of my heart to my family standing by me on all my journeys. To my twin sister, Farah, with whom I'm blessed to share every part of my life. To my mum, my believer, for putting a pen and paper in my hand. To my dad, my advocate and my absolute everything, for telling me I could write a book. Thank you.

Ameen.

Introduction

Belonging: what being included, visible and represented means to me

I was living in Brighton when I first came out as transgender. I remember that during LGBTQ Pride season, I went out in drag; I drew on a moustache, wore a binder to flatten my chest, stuffed a makeshift packer in my boxers to create a bulge between my legs and stepped into a masculinity that felt so natural to me. I would dance amongst dykes, lesbians, activists and feminists, who eventually all helped my transness make sense to me.

I was living with white housemates, white colleagues and white friends when I first came out as brown. I remember looking down at my brown hands, sitting in bed with my white partner on my white sheets and slowly and painfully realizing that the colour of my brown skin was never going to change, no matter what I thought. *I am always going to be brown; I am always going to be seen as brown; I am always going to be treated as brown. No matter what I think, see or feel, I am always going to be brown.*

It sounds obvious – I've been brown my whole life. I grew up in a brown family, in a brown town and I went to a brown school. It was also obvious that I was something else; not straight, not like other girls. I couldn't find the words. When I came out, I don't think I ever said the words. I followed the classic gay narrative: coloured my hair, got more piercings and moved to Brighton.

My family felt my move hard, and they felt I was moving away from more than just a place I called home. They acknowledged my queerness as a Western disease. They saw my expression as a rebellion against our brown roots, as if coming out was a way to be closer to white culture; as if I wanted to be queer, I had to be white. But the reality was that was exactly how I felt; I wanted to forget about my culture, which at the time I called backwards, oppressive and regressive. I wanted to forget that I would have to fight twice as hard to be seen, heard and loved. And living in a cis-normative, white-dominated queer sphere, it was easy to forget. It *is* easier to forget. I knew I wasn't white – despite how much I really wanted to be – but at the same time, I had forgotten that I was brown.

I remember scrolling through YouTube channels for videos of trans men who looked like me. Pakistani. South Asian. Brown. I didn't even know what to write in the search bar. No matter what I wrote, the search still came up with no results. Trans people of colour (TPOC) existed; I knew that. But where? And how? Instead, I took in as much detail as I could on all things transgender: every name change, every pronoun swap, every testosterone shot, every medical appointment, every before/after and pre-/post-photo series. I wanted to know exactly what this journey was going to be like for me. I was full with knowledge but the weight that sat in my stomach was heavy with worry.

I remember walking into a support group for trans men and listening to experiences of coming out as a trans man, all the name, gender and pronoun changes, every disowning and accepting family. As each person spoke, the weight in my stomach became heavier and heavier. I felt worried, scared and sad. I knew this was the support I needed: *this is my community, and I should feel connected to them. I should feel better now.* But I didn't.

Before I left, I took another look at everyone in the group and counted ten trans men. Ten white trans men. The worries in my head started to make sense: *my family just don't think about gender like this. These are new words; do they even exist in our language? They'll blame my friends, the media, this country; it doesn't matter if this is how I really feel.* My fears became real: *I can't leave my family even if they don't understand; they've given me so much and I can't just walk away from them. I don't want to disown them. I don't want to do this alone.*

I felt alone because all I knew was that *white* trans people existed. White milestones and white transitions and white narratives that just became *the* milestones everyone must reach, *the* way to transition and *the* only trans narrative. That just became *the* way to be trans. Through conversations with friends and medical professionals, I realized that the way I wanted to transition, away from the white gaze and Western norms, was not trans enough. I wasn't trans enough if I didn't change my name to an Anglo-sounding traditional male name. I wasn't trans enough if I stayed in touch with my family despite being misgendered often. I wasn't trans enough if I didn't take hormones, if medical transition wasn't a huge part of my trans identity. I wasn't trans enough as a person of colour.

It was desperation and isolation that led me to stand out and speak out, starting Facebook groups and laying foundations for queer and trans people of colour. And slowly, our community built up around it. In the spaces I accessed online and in real life, it became clear that trans people of colour are not visible, invisible and hypervisible. When visibility is synonymous with validity and existence, it makes me feel like people like me don't exist. Unfortunately, for centuries this has been the mission of the mainstream.

His/her/their-stories

When trans people of colour *are* visible, we are erased. Historically, our identities and experiences have been erased from cultural and historical accounts, with many believing gender fluidity is hard to find across Asia, Africa and the Americas. Trans people of colour exist outside of the English language and beyond the Western gaze as khwaja sera (Pakistan), hijra (India), bakla (Philippines), kathoey (Thailand), machi (Chile and Argentina), two-spirit (Native American and First Nations), berdarche (North America), xanith (Arabian peninsula) and more; we are many more. We exist and we have always existed.

> My ancestors were performers. In life. The earliest shamanic rituals involved women and men exchanging genders. Old, old rituals. Top-notch performances. Life and death stuff. We're talking cross-cultural here. We're talking rising way way

> way above being a man or a woman. That's how my ances-
> tors would fly. That's how my ancestors would talk with the
> goddesses and the gods. Old rituals. (Bornstein 1994, p.143)

Trans people are more than just a third gender. Evan B. Towle and Lynn M. Morgan (2006) discuss 'third gender' as a romanticization and reduction of non-Western non-binary identities, practices, terminologies and histories, building a 'West versus the rest' mentality. They add that using the 'third gender' concept in this way means it 'becomes a junk drawer into which a great non-Western gender miscellany is carelessly dumped' (p.676). Our understanding of gender diversity for people of colour diminishes, as does our awareness of gender oppression and as does the potential for gender liberation. Understanding, oppression and liberation are all linked. If we don't understand gender diversity in a way that is true and meaningful for non-Western cultures, we won't see the ways we stereotype and distort it, nor the way in which this upholds gender dynamics and oppressions from the West. We will be far from gender liberation.

It's bigger than just a junk drawer. 'The history of gender is interwoven with the history of colonialism', write Barker and Scheele (2019, p.12). 'Europeans from the 16th century onwards imposed their understandings of gender and family life on the people they colonized – as well as often wiping out indigenous groups, and their ways of doing gender.' Not only have non-Western gender identities been minimalized, they have been erased completely to fit the binary genders we understand in the West: male and female. These Western gender hierarchies have been spread and maintained across parts of the world that were colonized by Western empires, in particular by the British Empire, through oppressive laws and legislation. The British Empire introduced the criminalization of homosexuality across its colonies with the Buggery Act in 1533; homophobia was indeed an export of the British Empire (Hubbard, 2017). This shaped Section 377, which prosecuted homosexuality across Malaysia, Singapore, Pakistan, Bangladesh, Myanmar and Jamaica, where it still remains. Transgender and non-binary people continue to be prosecuted as gay men, as local gender identities and language around gender fluidity are ignored (Quah, 2020).

In South Asia, the British Empire introduced the Criminal Tribes Act (CTA) in 1871, controlling khwaja sera and hijra communities and pushing them further into poverty and social exclusion (Gul, 2018). Unfortunately, many faith leaders absorbed these colonial laws and norms as their own, enforcing them through conservative Islam and Hindi fundamentalism, so despite laws changing to protect third gender communities, there are many religious figures who still oppose them.

In addition to our colonial history, we must be aware of imperialism, that is, how we can reproduce it when we educate ourselves and others about these histories. I include myself in this, despite my South Asian heritage; I was born in England and have spent the majority of my life in Western societies. Towle and Morgan (2006, p.672) also talk about 'the pitfalls of primordialism', how through simplifying ancient histories and reducing gender diversity to a single third gender category that incorporates all non-Western non-binary identities, practices, terminologies and histories, we lose a lot. Gender diversity is not just history, it is living, moving, breathing and varied cultures. To understand our primordial lens, we need to look at our own society's gender politics, cultures and histories.

When trans people of colour *are* visible, we are targets. We face increased rates of violence, murder and suicide from the hypervisibility and lack of safety for our communities. In particular, trans women and trans-feminine people from Black and Latinx communities face the highest rates of harm. This is primarily due to the systems of transmisogyny and racism pervading health, law, media, police and state institutions that fail these communities and replicate these oppressions through violence. Visible trans people of colour are seen as such a threat that we are silenced and erased, which is notable in how little of our history is accessible. However, this is changing; as our community has more representation and voices than ever before, LGBTQ organizations are scrambling to include us too.

Buzzwords: the issue of inclusive practice within LGBTQ+ organizations and spaces

The first time I saw the word 'diversity' in an LGBTQ setting was when I applied for a job as a 'diversity worker' at an LGBTQ charity. What it meant to me at the time was that difference is acknowledged and celebrated. At the time, I needed to hear that. It was exciting for me to be employed but exciting for the charity for different reasons; with the post of just one worker, they could reach three different communities of BAME, disabled and faith youth, and tick three diversity boxes. The work for these communities stayed within these communities and this new diversity strand. It was an add-on project, which is often the case; however, the downside of add-on diversity projects is that they are not then embedded into the organization.

The projects can just as easily be removed, and the organization will continue to function as it was before, much to the detriment of the communities the project was serving.

It was also exciting for the charity for another reason; I was the only trans person of colour in their staff team. Their workforce became diverse, and that word became a smokescreen to cover the experience of being the only trans person of colour in a team and the reasons why the team lacked diversity in the first place.

I was also learning about intersectionality around the same time my workplace got hold of the word. I watched how intersectionality was used as a tool to show how different and multi-faceted everyone in the organization was, as opposed to examining why the difference is there in the first place. It was an exciting word that rid the organization of any responsibility of examining this, when that is what intersectionality is – looking at the intersections of power and oppression within identity. I started to see the many issues that permeated not just this charity but LGBTQ spaces as a whole:

- The issue that inclusive practice is sometimes too big a demand for an organization to place upon itself. Either the communities it is trying to reach are failed, or the staff and volunteers who are there to reach them are failed.

- The issue that exclusive organizations write inclusive practice themselves, replicating oppressions and then wondering why it isn't working.

- The issue that organizations fail on practising inclusivity within their organization and (re)building a workplace culture that lasts. It is just a word, a one-off awareness day or an optional training course.

Sitting on 'BAME steering groups' and facilitating numerous trans focus groups, I have witnessed these same issues arising, the same conversations being repeated and the same mistakes being made. Diversity is a smokescreen, intersectionality is a misused tool and inclusivity is not a practice, just a word. The issue of being 'the only...' in an organization is that there aren't many others who you can go to for support or even to find out that this is an issue happening everywhere; you aren't the only one.

Putting the T first: the relationship between gender and sexuality in LGBTQ

Something that was particularly important to me when writing this section was to keep gender separate from sexual orientation/sexuality and avoid tucking the T under the LGBTQ umbrella. Whilst sexuality and gender are related, they are separate identities. Often gender identity gets conflated with sexuality and orientation. When transgender identities are combined with lesbian, gay, bisexual and queer, they are often forgotten. When transgender identities are recognized, often people of colour are forgotten. Experiences of gender roles, expressions and identities within POC communities need to be separate from diverse sexualities in POC communities. In addition to this, it excludes the POC trans communities who do not relate to, are not attached to and do not identify with LGBTQ.

Exploring gender and sexuality separately is important because the way transphobia and transmisogyny operate also needs to be examined separately from homophobia and sexism. Different systems of oppression affect trans and gender-diverse communities, which do affect LGBTQ and cis communities, but often stem from anti-trans oppression that needs to be understood.

Existing research and information that I have found on LGBTQ POC communities overwhelmingly only represents gay men and lesbians, despite the use of the acronym LGBTQ, which implies trans people are included when they are not. Trans research is overwhelmingly white. Finding research that reportedly represents trans POC people has been disappointing; we are often an afterthought, an exception, a minority. Our community is not a minority, and when we are excluded, the trans, LGBTQ and POC community is not wholly included. Although I cannot say I have found all the research reflecting trans POC communities – there will continue to be missing gaps in trans POC literature – I can say that the questions it raises are ones we all need to hear. Who gets to hold power over trans POC knowledge, and who is sharing knowledge? Where are we able to share information safely and research appropriately into these communities? What does this reveal about how we research, record and honour these communities? These questions remind me how important it is to have trans POC people thought of at the very start, and why the T needs to come first.

About this book[1]

> Help the trans POC community – a minority within a minority. Our voices are not forgotten.
>
> – survey respondent

This book goes back to the beginning. It starts where we start, with our history, the forces that have shaped it and those who have continued to do so. It follows seven sections. In Section 1, I cover identity and intersectionality, terminology, language and the power of language, touching on history and usage. There's a particular focus on things we can't say and why we can't say them, intersectionality theory, shame and white and cis privilege, ending on the experiences of trans people of colour in the UK.

Section 2, Creating a Safe(r) Space, explores the use of 'safe' vs 'safer', the privilege of safety, free speech and censorship, exclusionary spaces, accessible spaces and gender-inclusive spaces that are more than just toilets. Section 3, Holding a Safe(r) Space, starts with intersectionality theory to cover deeper understandings of racism, gender diversity, sex diversity and class. This section also includes building agreements,

---

1   After supporting Samir Jeraj at the Race Equality Foundation with research on BAME trans experiences (Jeraj, 2014), I connected with Terry and Bernard Reed at GIRES, who have published fact sheets on trans experiences and identities and keep an online database of trans organizations in the UK: TranzWiki. We created a BAME trans fact sheet (The National LGB&T Partnership, n.d.) and partnered together to write a guide titled 'Inclusivity: supporting BAME trans people' (Choudrey, 2016) to address what inclusive practice looks like for these communities. This is how this book came to be.

how to be accountable when mistakes are made and how to maintain a safe space.

Section 4 is about putting this into practise, starting with a cautionary note on looking intersectional versus being intersectional. From online, physical and visible presence, this offers questions to reflect on, with specific notes on making advertising, recruitment, partnership and funding inclusive too. In Section 5, I explore ways to celebrate and commemorate trans people of colour (TPOC) communities, from national and international celebrations and awareness days to history months and Pride and drawing up an annual calendar. This section ends on the meaning and importance of the Black Lives Matter movement for our communities.

Section 6 on exclusion and inclusion uses real-life examples from anonymous survey respondents and the many LGBTQ POC communities and organizations that are showcasing inclusion and challenging exclusion to suggest what we can learn moving forward. I also provide a list of ten ways to make your practice inclusive, and I give you my concluding thoughts in Section 7.

You'll read quotes of experiences from participants of my anonymous survey as well as research findings and quotes I've taken from as many LGBTQ, trans, intersex, queer, Black, people of colour, disabled, faith and UK-based researchers, writers and community activists as I can. I acknowledge that my voice is just one voice and I represent just one part of the trans POC community. My own thoughts on inclusive practice will be inherently exclusive as they come from my own gaze, which is why it's important to me that there are many others speaking on this and that they have been included. It's not about collecting *different* voices but collecting *more* voices. I struggle with naming without fragmenting, without excluding,' writes Anzaldúa (1998). This writing is investigation and education. This writing is not trans, POC, or British Asian. Putting myself into a marginalized box puts the words that I'm writing into a marginalized box; this writing isn't for marginalized people. This is for everyone. To quote the author and activist adrienne maree brown (2017): 'While my default position is wonder, I am not without critique, disappointment, frustration and even depression when I contemplate humanity.'

When I proposed this book, the first question I asked myself was 'Why does this book exist?' I hope it is clear by now. This book exists because we do.

Section 1

Identity and Intersectionality

The meanings of identity and intersectionality can get lost amongst theory or simplified, meaning our multi-dimensional experiences are lost or simplified to just one experience. Single-issue politics are comfortable for organizations and mainstream society, but they're dangerous. **'There is no such thing as a single-issue struggle because we do not live single-issue lives'**, said Audre Lorde (1982). Our lives are complex, multi and plenty; we must be held in our entirety.

Terminology

When I deliver training on gender diversity, my terminology slide is blank. This is intentional.

Language is changing all the time. I believe that it is more important that we understand that than that we understand what a certain word means. To try and cover every term that would come under gender diversity would require more than just a slide and more than just one training. To try and define every term that we will encounter around gender is impossible – there's a lot I can share from what I know, and there is so much more that I don't know.

It's not just language that changes – of course there are new words and new acronyms, but the meanings also change as our contexts and cultures change. Language changes in different cultures and global contexts; some words aren't translatable in certain languages and others simply do not exist. Once the journey of words can be understood, the needs and experiences of those communities can be understood better too. Language is incredibly personal too, and what one word means to one person may differ to another. These are some of the reasons why language can be so beautiful and so powerful. If we approach language like this, as fluid and not fixed, it can give us more room for our own practice.

This time, however, I have not left the terminology section blank. I have included it as you have already been introduced to terms that exist in a specific context, such as 'people of colour' and 'trans'. I want to also take this time to explain why I am choosing to use certain words and what they mean in the context of these pages.

BAME – Black, Asian and minority ethnic

This is a term used as a classification of ethnic communities and so-called 'minorities' in the UK. It has come from the government and remains a categorization tool used when capturing most demographic data, such as in the census. When I first started writing this book, I was using the term 'BAME'.

As time has gone on and conversations around race have evolved, more and more people reject 'BAME', including me.

One of the criticisms is how often and how easily Black is conflated with BAME. Statistics that speak for BAME populations sometimes don't include any Black communities. Events that claim to represent BAME people don't include any Black organizers. Black voices and Black experiences are overlooked. Acronyms can be convenient, but all too often they hide what really needs paying attention to (Joseph, 2020).

POC – person/people of colour

This is an acronym, pronounced as the word 'pock' or initialized as 'P.O.C.'. This is used to describe anyone who is not white. Its origins are American; however, it's been adopted in the UK, starting in activist communities as an alternative to BAME. In America, it has historically been used by Black leaders and activists to bring all non-white people together to fight racism.

Again, this as an acronym is often used interchangeably with Black people despite the intentions of building solidarity across non-white people. Some avoid this by using the acronym 'BPOC' – Black and people of colour. 'BIPOC' is used by some communities to include Indigenous peoples as another group that is ignored.

These are intentional acts to ensure these voices do not get overlooked, emphasizing their different experiences and acknowledging the historical oppressions they have faced compared to other non-white people. Whilst the definition of 'POC' is not explicitly about colour per se, some criticize that the term is inherently reflective of skin colour and placed in contrast to whiteness. Other criticisms include some not knowing who is 'allowed' to call themselves a person of colour. Those using 'POC' can further marginalize the very communities they are seeking to unite.

> The term 'people of colour' is progress from harmful racial terms that were previously used such as 'coloured', but again why is the benchmark of humanity whiteness?
>
> It is the standard by which everybody else is measured and defined.
>
> It is the default, the primary, beyond this definition lives the 'other'.
>
> The 'non-white'.
>
> The 'person of colour'.
>
> Is this really progressive?
>
> Helpful?
>
> Politically correct?
>
> Inclusive? (Adamson, 2020)

It has evolved from our communities, for our communities. I'm using it here as a term acknowledging its origins and that it carries historical and systemic oppression with it. In these pages, I include all non-white people when I write people of colour or POC, and to recognize the differences in experiences and oppressions faced by our communities, I will explicitly write Black people or non-Black people of colour (for more on why this is capitalized, see 'Language').

Queer

'Queer' was an insult, a homophobic slur used against gay and trans people, and it still is in some places. Now it has been reclaimed by the very communities it intended to oppress. 'Queer' carries this history with it; it's an empowering, political word to many, including me. It doesn't define my gender nor the gender of people I am attracted to; what it means for someone is personal. Some use 'queer' synonymously with 'gay' and 'LGBT'; however, some see 'queer' as separate due to its painful history or political connotations. This word doesn't define every LGBTQ person and that must be remembered; another word chosen for us, by us.

LGBTQ – lesbian, gay, bisexual, trans, queer

There are many different variations of this acronym dependant on the context and person using it.

Some add an 'A' for 'asexual'; some add an 'I' for intersex, and there are many more. To acknowledge these identities and the many more identities beyond our knowledge, others just add a plus sign: 'LGBT+'. I will be using the version 'LGBTQ' to talk about all communities that have sexual and gender diversity.

QTIPOC – queer, trans, intersex person/people of colour

This is an acronym pronounced 'cutie-pock', which is becoming more widely used when talking about LGBTQ people of colour. As with POC, it's a political and significant term coined by our communities, for our communities. Sometimes written 'QTPOC' (queer and trans people of colour) or 'QTIBPOC' (queer, trans, intersex, Black and people of colour) depending on the context and person using it.

Cis

This is shorthand for 'cisgender' and refers to someone who identifies with the sex they were assigned at birth; their gender identity is the same as their sex. The prefix 'cis' comes from Latin, meaning 'on the same side'. This not a slur, nor does it carry any stigma or political or historical prejudice. Its use has led to some rejection from cisgender men and women simply because it's a lesser known term that hasn't historically been used. Now 'cisgender' is recognized by the Oxford Dictionary. As our understanding of gender expands, the language of gender will follow.

Trans

This refers to someone who doesn't identify with the sex they were assigned at birth. The prefix 'trans' comes from Latin, meaning 'across'. This is an umbrella term used for all transgender, gender non-conforming and non-binary identities. However, not all gender non-conforming and non-binary people like to be called trans; to make this distinction, some write 'trans and non-binary' or 'T & NB' explicitly. Non-binary is another umbrella term for all identities outside of the gender binary (see below). The lists of words that come under these two umbrellas are endless, infinite and completely personal.

Non-binary

This is an umbrella term for all gender identities that do not fit the gender binary of man and woman/male and female – they are not binary. There are lots of different words used to define people who have no gender (agender), are somewhere between genders (androgyne), are both genders or multiple genders (bigender or pangender), are another gender completely (third gender) or are a gender that moves between many (gender fluid). Sometimes 'non-binary' is abbreviated as 'NB' – pronounced 'enby' – and also can be written as 'enby'. Again, this is a personal preference, and the words that people use can be just that, or they can be wholly political aimed to challenge the binary (genderqueer or genderfuck).

Intersex

This the last of the umbrella terminologies. This term holds the variety of differences where a person does not fit the sex binary of male or female. It refers to anatomical differences to do with sex traits and reproductive anatomy: that's genitals, hormones, chromosomes and more – it's a natural variation of biological sex. Because of the diversity in variations, some intersex traits are noticed at birth, some at puberty through development and others much later in life. There is still so much stigma and shame around intersex infants, leading to non-consensual medical interventions on babies, forcing them to fit into either male or female. These unnecessary and life-changing decisions are made on behalf of young people whose sex traits appear different. Intersex communities worldwide are campaigning for an end to pathologizing intersex traits as disorders that need fixing and for a ban on non-consensual intersex infant surgery.

Intersex is not a gender identity – some intersex people are transgender and some are cisgender (see 'Understanding sex diversity' in Section 3 for more). Because some intersex people are transgender and/or LGBQ, it is sometimes included under the LGBTQ umbrella. I've included it here because whilst they fight for recognition, appropriate healthcare and bodily autonomy, the differences are critical and must stop being conflated with trans identities. As this book is written by someone who is not intersex (endosex), this isn't writing on inclusive intersex practice; however it will include how trans communities can practise intersex solidarity.

Language

Defining words around gender is quite a task. It's easy to get lost and weighed down by words we don't know, but it's clear how important and meaningful the words we use are. When it comes to how it's written here, I'm using 'trans' for the wide umbrella and full spectrum of all gender identities that come under it, including non-binary, intersex and gender non-conforming people. Where texts or issues relate to non-binary people or intersex people, for example, I will take care to make this explicit.

The key points to take away here are:

- Language is changing all the time, evolving as we are, across time, between generations and within communities. Open the glossary of another gender book and this list will look different.

- If you are in any doubt, simply don't use that word you're unsure about ('Are you non-binary?'), ask the person/group directly ('What is your gender identity?') or just google it ('How do I respectfully ask someone about their gender?').

- Explore your own language around gender. Question where (or who) these words have come from. Educate yourself on the history of language, including the politics and activism behind it. Keep checking with communities – listen to the words they use, don't wait to be informed and update your own vocabulary.

Of course, there will be a time when we have used alternative wording, have asked someone their preferences, given an open question, done the learning by ourselves and still get it wrong. I initially thought of a sharing a list of 'what not to say': another terminology section of 'wrong' terms that are outdated, offensive and stigmatizing. However, to repeat some of those words and have them be read doesn't feel the most considerate approach nor does being told what's wrong without explanation. Getting it wrong is part of the learning process. Instead of trying to avoid getting it wrong, we can prepare ourselves for when we do and understand why it's not right.

Why can't I say that? It's my right

For some, not being able to say something can feel like a violation of their freedom of speech where 'everyone has the right to freedom of expression' (*Human Rights Act, 1998*). The UK laws uphold this legislation as well as outlaw hate speech (Section 4 of the *Public Order Act, 1986*) and protects people from discrimination (*Equality Act, 2010*). How these laws are enforced and acted on could be a separate issue; the point remains that where free speech becomes harmful, hatred or oppressive, it becomes a violation of others.

> *REFLECT ON*
> - Why does it matter so much to say something harmful, hateful or oppressive?
> - Can you use another word instead of something derogatory to express your point?

But they say that in this other part of the world

What we hear here in the UK will be different to what we hear around the world. It doesn't even have to be another part of the world; it could be a different part of the country or a different community where you can find new language, or old language used in different ways. This is a reflection on gender, geography, race, class and more – all of these influence language. By bringing up the context of somewhere else, we're dismissing the experiences of the people and history around us, again just for the right to say a word that we can't say.

> *REFLECT ON*
> - What is stopping you from listening to the people or communities around you?

They call themselves that and said it's okay for me to say it

Language is personal, and what we call ourselves is just that: personal. This is why some words fit us better than others and why other words make us uncomfortable. Pay attention to the discomfort. If you don't feel okay about saying something even after someone has given permission for you to say it, you can still decline respectfully and explain why it's not appropriate for you or explore this privately. Some words should only be used by the people who that word applies to, whether that is a reclaimed word or a word in another language. Even when we have the permission of one person to use a word, we have to consider the other people who also use that word. One person does not speak for a whole community. This is especially important when we are outside of a community we don't share an identity with, although of course it happens within communities too. There will be differences in opinions, and the important thing is to hold this in mind.

REFLECT ON

- Am I assuming everyone who uses this word would feel okay about me using it and generalizing a community?
- Instead of seeking permission to use this word, could I use an alternative word?

It was okay to say it back then; you know what I mean

The way language captures history so well is in how it changes across time. Words are on a journey like a river, and a river never stays the same. There are many words beyond identity and beliefs that have evolved over centuries, trickling through the mainstream to sub-streams making room for new words to flow through. One of the ways this can be explored is through tracing words back to their origins and finding derogatory or oppressive roots. We can see this where the origins of words are medical, used primarily to diagnose mental disorders that have since been removed from use, become outdated or been reworded as we understand difference better. However, 'back then' the context was not exactly neutral, even in the medical field. Words reflect the culture at the time; where a culture is ableist, racist or homophobic, the language will reflect this. When we say something was okay to say in a previous time or generation, we are saying it was okay to be ableist, racist or homophobic and it's okay to continue being like that. We perpetuate values and prejudice whenever we use an outdated word, when we refuse to correct ourselves or seek what to say instead.

REFLECT ON

- What makes it difficult to adopt a new language? Is this limited to identity, politics or something specific?
- Was something really okay to say 'back then' or amongst another generation, or was discrimination just more normalized?

Do you mean politically or with a capital B?

The term 'Black' has had a journey across generations, and its usage is still evolving today. In activist and organizer circles fighting against racism in the 1970s in the UK, the term 'political blackness' was common. However, for as long as 'political blackness' has been used, there has been push back against it. As the term suggests, it is a political tool used to unite people of colour against racism, but in trying to unite communities of colour, it has alienated them.

> One key contention with political blackness is that it doesn't account for anti-black attitudes among people of colour who are not of African descent... I'm not usually the one calling for unity, and I think it has to be done carefully here, so as not to flatten differences or ignore existing discrimination. But it's really clear to me that there needs to be some inter-generational dialogue. There may never be a consensus on political blackness, but we could learn a lot from each other. (Eddo-Lodge, 2018b)

When it comes to how the word is written, many give the reasoning that 'black' with a lowercase 'b' is simply a colour, whereas 'Black' with a capital 'B' is an ethnicity, culture and community of people from the African diaspora. This has also been recognized by the Associated Press, who now capitalize 'Black' but not 'white', an acknowledgement of history and the disproportionate experiences of racial discrimination carried through 'Black'. 'Capitalizing the term white, as is done by white supremacists, risks subtly conveying legitimacy to such beliefs', explains John Daniszewski, vice president of the Associated Press (Bauder, 2020).

Where it is written here, 'Black' will be capitalized and 'white' will not to reflect the history and culture of the African diaspora as distinct from that of white people. I acknowledge my position and my privilege, as someone from neither community, that I do not know the direct impact of this language.

Whatever language we use, it isn't enough to just say the right thing. We have to do the right thing.

To illustrate the impact of gender discrimination and racial bias on language, I've included the voices of trans authors Alex Iantaffi and Meg-John Barker as well as R. Kaur from the POC-led organization Charity So White.

The importance of language by Alex Iantaffi and Meg-John Barker

- The impact of language is subtle but almost always favours men by default. However, small semantic changes will make a big difference from including women and trans people in a dialogue to removing barriers to other spaces, and overall increasing a sense of confidence and belonging:

  > Language often shapes our experience more than we realise. For example, when the generic 'man' is used to mean human, as in 'mankind' or 'every man for himself' people who are not men often don't remember what has been said as well, and experience lowers confidence afterwards than when inclusive language like 'human' or 'person' is used. This can become a barrier to learning in education, or wellbeing in healthcare. (Iantaffi and Barker, 2018, p.34)

- The beauty of language is pertinent through trans experiences towards understanding ourselves. There is a hugely positive and validating impact from language that mustn't be forgotten either:

> Language enables different – often more positive – experiences. For example, for many trans and/or non-binary people, finding that there is a word that feels like a good fit for them is part of what enables themselves in ways that feel congruent and comfortable, as well as helping them to explain their experience to others. Having a shared language for something can make it feel more legitimate and understandable. (Iantaffi and Barker, 2018, pp.34–35)

- The power of language is why it's such an important place to start (for more on the benefits and challenges of 'X-only' spaces, see Section 2):

> Language can be used to include or exclude people. To respect or to reject them. For example sometimes it can feel very valuable for a marginalised group to have an 'X-only' space (e.g. bisexual-only, or people-of-colour-only) where they can talk about some of their experiences in relative safety with people who share these experiences. On the other hand, exclusive policies can easily divide and fragment communities, such as women's events that don't welcome trans women often using problematic language to define who 'counts' as a woman. (Iantaffi and Barker, 2018, p.35)

Language barriers: how our words obscure bias and discrimination (Kaur, 2020)

We can come to understand language as more than just words; it's a method of communication, a tool for understanding ourselves, an archive that marks history and time and a mirror that reflects the society we are in, including the bias that otherwise goes unseen. If we can face the mirror, we can hear that 'I don't think you're ready for the next step', 'We need to be objective and neutral about this' and 'Wow, you really know your stuff don't you?' are all ways bias is hidden, as Kaur explains from her own experiences:

- **Language is one of the subtle ways in which modern forms of bias and discrimination are exercised in the sector.** It helps to ensure the right people *fit in* and *profit* from the opportunities available in a sector.

- **The messages communicated through these phrases are inauthentic, they tend to generate false expectations which often lead to confusion and friction.** I have especially found this to be the case when working specifically in the social innovation sector. Here, organisations operate with deeply hierarchical power structures but pretend to have 'flat' cultures where apparently 'everyone has an equal voice' – as a woman of colour I have found these organisations highly confusing to navigate.

- **The intention behind using neutral/constructive language is so cleverly disguised that people can't even challenge it – that's how insidious it is – yet everyone is smart enough to read between the lines.**

- Using language in this way is helping a sector focussed on addressing social challenges to **nurture workplace cultures that are exclusive, homogenous and – perpetually – privileged.**

(Kaur, 2020)

Intersectionality

Everyone has multiple identities and experiences that make them who they are. Intersectionality is the theory that connects these parts together (see Figure 1.1).

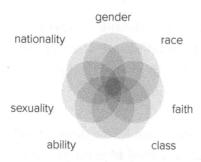

gender

nationality   race

sexuality   faith

ability   class

Figure 1.1 How the different parts of our identities overlap with each other

Kimberlé Crenshaw, an American lawyer and scholar, coined the term 'intersectionality' to describe the experience of different types of oppression, specifically those faced by black women. Crenshaw illustrates this by talking about moving traffic:

> Consider an analogy to traffic in an intersection, coming and going in all four directions. Discrimination, like traffic through an intersection, may flow in one direction, and it may flow in another. If an accident happens in an intersection, it can be caused by cars traveling from any number of directions and, sometimes, from all of them. Similarly, if a Black woman is harmed because she is in an intersection, her injury could result from sex discrimination or race discrimination. (Crenshaw, 1989, p.149)

Talking about sexism and racism as separate issues means that the experiences faced by Black women are erased, as are the experiences of people who face multiple oppressions across different identities. An intersectional approach recognizes that these multiple identities exist in multiple combinations, which means that all voices are included at one time.

These identities include gender and race, as this book will cover, but can also include identities around faith or religion, nationality, citizenship or immigration status, socio-economic class, sexuality, age and dis/ability.

From this we can examine the different oppressions and discriminations a person faces by looking at the intersections of oppression. For example, a Muslim non-binary person with Bengali heritage will experience racism, transphobia and Islamophobia together; their gender non-conformity will be visible at the same time as their skin colour. Their heritage, visible through their name or appearance, may denote their Islamic faith. Their oppressions are all connected, and all oppression is connected. Intersectionality encourages solidarity and work together across communities, strengthening our fight against oppression.

> I find it awkward when I'm only framed as a transgender rights activist – I'm a Black trans woman, I'm a Black feminist. (Kuchenga interviewed in 'Trans through time' by Unfinished Business podcast (The British Library 2021))

Oppression also requires oppressors. Prejudice requires power. Not only can we experience oppression across these identity strands, we can also experience privilege. Depending on how our upbringing, cultural or societal norms influence our identities, we can be in a position of power. For example, a white, able-bodied trans man with British citizenship will face oppression based on his gender identity; however his race, nationality and able body will grant him a position of privilege, where he does not face oppression but holds power across these parts of his identity. His identities intersect with each other constantly as his contexts change. The world around him can read him as an able-bodied white man or as a trans man or as someone else as another part of his identity is disclosed, such as his class background.

> Analyzing an instance of injustice as *solely* racial, gendered or economic in nature is likely to result in an inadequate understanding of causes, injuries and solutions. No one particular form of oppression, for example, sexism, is necessarily the root cause for, or automatically more urgent to address than another. (Juang, 2006, p.709)

Taking an intersectional approach requires us to be mindful of the complexities of people, and respectful of the intersecting identities that are visible, hidden and contextual. Intersectionality means understanding and celebrating the diversity of our communities, and within organizations it means fair representation and safe spaces for everyone.

> In other words, there is a link between identity privileges, and our negotiation of them, on the one hand, and discrimination, on the other. Our identities are reflective and constitutive of systems of oppression. Racism requires white privilege. Sexism requires male privilege. Homophobia requires heterosexual privilege. The very intelligibility of our identities is their association, or lack thereof, with privilege. This creates an

obligation on the part of those of us with privileged identities to expose and to challenge them. (Carbado, 2005, p.191)

Mamta Accapadi (2007) talks about 'one up/one down' identities – that is one identity that is privileged and another that is oppressed – and how we must recognize when the privileged identity is the operating norm. For example, if you are white and a woman, you must recognize the power that comes with your whiteness, the norm.

She says 'All of our social identities inform and shape one another. One's identity as a woman is shaped by multiple factors in her life, including race, social class, sexual orientation, and so on. While sexism shapes the nature of womanhood, White womanhood looks very different than Asian American, Black, Indigenous, or Latina womanhood, because each woman's experience is shaped by the internal expectations and external perceptions of what it means to be a woman within each of these racial communities' (Accapadi, 2007, p.209).

These systems exist due to the power held by dominant groups of a society. The voices that dominate our society have been in power for generations, and the systems and structures have been built on this power. This means that the systems that we function in automatically benefit those already in power. These systems also protect those in power. In the context of these pages and the UK today, white people and cis people hold institutional power. The systems of white supremacy, racism, anti-Blackness, cis-normativity (the belief that a person's gender identity matches the sex/gender assigned at birth and that they are cisgender), cissexism (the belief that cis people's genders, identities and expressions are the norm and thus more legitimate than those of trans people) and transphobia are upheld in our society unless we are aware of our own position within it and take action to combat this. One of the first things we can do is understand our privilege.

Naming it

Before we dive into privilege, there's something I want to name: it's shame. It sneaks its way in when we are understanding new experiences and learning about identities and can play a role when we are interacting with people full stop.

Shame is such a powerful emotion in that it has a tremendous emotional, mental and physical impact on us. It can also be traumatic – shame literally creates the same physiological response as a traumatic event. If you think about a time you felt shame, can you remember what happened in your body? Did your skin temperature change? Did you feel sweat under your arms or did your mouth turn dry? Our reactions can be attributed to a fight, flight or freeze response. Shame makes us want to attack, run away or do nothing.

Dr Brené Brown (2020) an American professor and author, has researched this topic for years, including writing on shame resilience theory (2006), presenting a TED talk, 'Listening to Shame' (2012) and engaging in various discourses on preventing shame spirals and empathy as the antidote to shame. For now, I'm just going to give us a starting point. It's her two-step shame primer.

'One: we all have it'

We all have shame, and we are all capable of feeling shame.

Shame is not reserved for certain communities; shame does not understand hierarchies or privilege. No matter what our identity or experiences of culture, we all have shame. I believe that as long as oppression exists, so will shame; as we internalize oppression, our shame will turn inwards. We need liberation in our lives to free ourselves from shame and internalized oppression. Shame does have a function to protect us, but only when nothing else will.

'Two: no one likes to talk about it'

It wouldn't surprise me if this is uncomfortable, maybe even painful – reading about shame can be just as unpleasant as talking about it. But we must talk about shame. We have to name it, witness it and tolerate it; we can't escape it because it will stay within.

Aside from how it might make us physically and emotionally feel, why don't we like to talk about it? The undercurrents of shame are often deep fears or a judgement about who we are as people. 'I am a bad person. I am unlovable.' Or unvaluable, undesirable, unlikeable. We don't want to believe these things, and shame hands us the proof. We're scared, and if we talk about it, we risk feeling it, which stop us from making a change. Even though I believe we are all good people, deserving of love, trying our best. Shame arrives and destroys all that.

'Shame needs three things'

Shame needs three things to grow exponentially: secrecy, silence and judgement. (Brown, 2020)

Inclusive practice needs to find ways to counter these things. To be transparent, to be vocal and to be open. By understanding shame, we can make change effective, meaningful and long lasting.

Before we name shame, we need a language so that we're able to talk about it.

Before we talk about shame, we need a place to start that conversation.

Before we find a place, we need to build trust, to have empathy in our shame and find community to hold it.

We simply have to talk about shame. We can't continue this without talking about it. Our practice can't be inclusive if we don't understand shame and guilt. The two are linked and often conflated, but they're different. Brown (2020) says, 'Shame is "I am bad", guilt is "I did something bad".' Understanding the difference between character and behaviour is massive when it comes to taking action and making mistakes.

Untangling oppression is messy. There are many roadblocks to overcome, and one of the things that stops us is ourselves. So getting to know ourselves is key. How does it make you feel when you try and fail or when you get something wrong and someone calls you out?

For example, consider when a person of colour makes someone aware of their white privilege as a factor in their successes or their escaping of harm. Phrases like white guilt, white silence and white fragility might come to mind. All of these are reactions that play on those fears of being a 'bad' person. These responses can potentially lead to a growth in shame by us wanting to cover it up, stay silent and judge others or persecute ourselves – more roadblocks in the path to making change happen.

What I call generally 'oppressor guilt' should not play a big part in owning privilege and using it in inclusive practice. Of course we are human and have emotional reactions to situations of injustice, especially when we play a part we didn't realize we had. But the opposite of shame is not privilege. Having privilege should not bring us shame but perspective. The quicker we move through our oppressor guilt, the quicker we will gain perspective.

White privilege

White privilege exists. It exists because racial discrimination exists. Often when we are taught about racism, we aren't taught about the mechanism of oppression. We are taught that it's mean to pick on people because of their skin colour. We aren't taught why people are discriminated against for their skin colour, and the reasons behind why white people discriminated against Black people and people of colour is spoken of in the past tense. This is one of the ways in which privileges continue to be invisible – they aren't named or acknowledged because the mechanism of racism is often misunderstood. This is how white people continue to benefit from the oppression of people of colour and the system of white supremacy is preserved.

> White privilege is an absence of the consequences of racism. An absence of structural discrimination, an absence of your race being viewed as a problem first and foremost. (Eddo-Lodge, 2018a, p.86)

The first step to fighting racism is not understanding racism;

it is understanding white privilege. Robin DiAngelo, academic and author of *White Fragility* (2018), writes 'Racism is a white problem. It was constructed and created by white people and the ultimate responsibility lies with white people. For too long we've looked at it as if it were someone else's problem, as if it was created in a vacuum. I want to push against that narrative' (Iqbal, 2019).

Peggy McIntosh, an American feminist scholar, has spent decades on equity, justice and anti-racism. Through her understandings of male privilege being protected and unacknowledged, and the interlocking hierarchies in society, she questioned whether as a white person she experienced white privilege; 'I had been taught about racism as something that puts others at a disadvantage but had been taught not to see one of its corollary aspects, white privilege, which puts me at an advantage' (1988).

McIntosh wrote about her experiences in an autobiographical essay, 'White Privilege and Male Privilege: A Personal Account of Coming to See Correspondences through Work in Women's Studies' (1988), which has been edited under 'White Privilege: Unpacking the Invisible Knapsack' (1989). This explores her personal experiences as a white person navigating a world with these unearned advantages, where privilege is something invisible and weightless carried like we would carry a rucksack full of special provisions, maps, passports, codebooks, visas, clothes, tools and blank cheques that would give us access to different parts of the world. McIntosh writes a list of the daily effects of white privilege in her own life, acknowledging whilst unpacking that she once took each experience for granted.

Unpacking white privilege increases understanding of

whiteness as an asset and awareness of the (unearned) power that comes with it. It reveals how little needs to be spoken about or seen of white privilege for it to benefit white people, and this in fact is how it functions.

I recommend reading McIntosh's full paper available for free at The National SEED Project, it is about her experience alone, however it is a useful starting point to make the invisible visible. Please make sure you have a space to reflect afterwards either by yourself or by speaking with someone who faces similar privileges (not a person of colour or anyone who is on the other side of the statement; they do not need to know how having white privilege makes you feel, as people of colour experience it daily). Take your time, find a paper or document to write, scribble, type, draw, react however you want.

Learning about your own privilege for the first time can be awkward, enraging, embarrassing or uncomfortable, and that's okay; it's a natural reaction to something you may not have chosen. Even if it's not the first time, it can still feel uncomfortable to be reminded of. It also may not be as simple as a statement; there are nuances to context and personal situations as there are multiplicities to our identities. However, these nuances don't withdraw the unasked benefits of white privilege. McIntosh adds that the word 'privilege' is misleading – it sounds like a good thing, something we've chosen, when actually we might not have asked for it, and often we don't. I agree, privilege exists simply because we do. And truthfully, privilege is not a special provision or an advantage. It is simply the way everyone should be treated.

When I talk about white privilege, I don't mean that white people have it easy, that they've never struggled, or that

> they've never lived in poverty. But white privilege is the fact
> that if you're white, your race will almost certainly positively
> impact your life's trajectory in some way. And you probably
> won't even notice it. (Eddo-Lodge, 2018a, p.87)

Cis privilege

McIntosh's writings on white privilege have inspired other scholars and activists to build tools to explore the everyday ways our many privileges benefit our lives through truly understanding the experiences of those who face oppression. Julia Serano, author of *Whipping Girl* (2007, p.161), writes: 'Gender variant people are oppressed by a system that forces everyone to identify and be easily recognisable as either a woman or a man.' Cis people's experiences are dominant in that it's assumed that everyone feels comfortable with the sex they were assigned at birth and the gender they were born and raised into. It's assumed that everyone cis people meet is cis; their ideology serves to validate and affirm their own experiences. The benefit of privilege is that it tells you your experience is universal.

Cedar (2008) and CPT (2019) have compiled similar material for cisgender people to recognize how their privilege affects their lives, making their experiences different from transgender, non-binary and gender non-conforming people. I have shared a sample of ten statements, adapted to a UK context (from American). To echo Cedar's preface not to argue with privilege lists: 'If you read them from a standpoint of wanting to deny your privilege, you'll come out having success-fully denied it but learning nothing. Read sympathetically and think about it. If there's something that seems like a privilege not all cis people have, try to consider why someone would put it on the list, what larger scale patterns I might be pointing to, rather than just rejecting it whole cloth.'

1. The sex/gender dichotomy does not have consequences in my life.

2. My gender is acknowledged universally, immediately and without hesitation.

3. I expect my gender to not unjustifiably affect my ability to travel internationally as my gender is represented and legal in all countries.

4. Bodies like mine are represented in the media and the arts. It is easily possible for representations of my naked body to pass restrictions and social media community guidelines.

5. My birth certificate, driver's license and passport are correct from the moment I get them.

6. My preferences for my gender have been honoured my whole life, by my doctors/GP, my parents/caregivers, my teachers, my relatives/extended family, my class-mates, my employers, etc.

7. If someone is uncertain about how I am gendered, they are likely to use their own criteria that will influence them to choose the gender that I identify with, as opposed to the gender that I actually identify with and am.

8. I expect be referred to respectfully without stating my preferences, or even being asked, no matter where I go, how I dress or whom I'm talking to. If this does not happen, whatever level of anger I express will be acceptable, and the offence will be immediately corrected.

9. My gender, and my access to gender-segregated facilities, gender-specific services and medical care, are upheld no matter how important or unimportant I consider my gender to be.

10. My right to inhabit my currently chosen gender is universally considered valid, regardless of my gendered behaviour as a child, or how I felt about being forced into the gender I inhabited then.

> **REFLECT ON**
>
> - What factors have you never thought of before?
> - Which statement made you think most?
> - How can your understanding of this improve your existing relationships with yourself and others?

If you do not see yourself as part of the problem, you cannot be part of the solution. (Saad, 2018, p.43)

Experiences of trans people of colour in the UK

Trans people of colour occupy communities beyond those just for trans people and those just for people of colour. It's important that we hear from a range of voices and remember that trans people of colour belong to different identity groups and communities. This shouldn't be a foundation for believing our experiences nor seen as evidence that racism and transphobia exist – we should be believed, and the evidence is much bigger than just us – but this should be a foundation for solidarity and how to support us better.

Anecdotal evidence of TPOC lives in the UK is becoming more freely available as technology and social media allow us to build our own platforms and speak directly with people, and with mainstream media we are represented more in storylines by diverse characters played by diverse actors. Generally, we are more visible, therefore we have more opportunity to be understood. In addition to this, racial injustices at the hands of police brutality, the disproportionate impact of Covid-19 for people of colour and the massive setbacks to trans healthcare have all shone a light in 2020 as to what our communities are experiencing and have been experiencing for decades. I've gathered direct writings and extracts from TPOC and TPOC research – our experiences are out there, and I encourage you to look further. Whilst some elements of our experiences are shared, these people are really expressing what it's like to be them and only them. When we read about an experience of a trans person of colour, we have simply read the experience of one trans person of colour.

On criminal justice[1]

Racism has been identified as another significant cause of negative interactions between police and trans people, especially Black trans people. TRANSforming Futures (Hord and Medcalf, 2020a) held a series of workshops with trans participants and some exclusively with trans POC participants to share their experiences of the criminal justice system and healthcare. The intersection between gender and race, and how that impacted expressions of racism, was repeatedly raised within the trans people of colour workshops.

Trans people of colour are already disproportionately criminalized because of racial profiling. Trans-masculine POC in particular report being followed around in shops by people who suspect they are stealing and being stopped by police more often if they are perceived as masculine.

TPOC participants:

- 'With the criminal justice system, colour comes first. If I ever experienced a hate crime, I wouldn't feel comfortable reporting it.'

- 'As long as you are white and a citizen then all your rights are in full effect. Otherwise, as TPOC, you don't have the same rights and are treated as a second-class citizen.'

---

1   Key messages adapted from TRANSforming Futures 'Trans people's experience of the criminal justice system in England' (Hord and Medcalf, 2020a).

- 'I'm almost always racially profiled and now that I'm trans it's even worse.'

- 'In this current quarantine situation, I've seen LGBT+ (generally white) people reminding people to be calling the police still – for instance on people not sticking to lockdown...with absolutely no awareness of how the police aren't to be trusted for many people, aren't accessible in the same way; that many are of the opinion that they're a racist, homophobic, transphobic institution.'

On healthcare[2]

Trans people of colour suggested that TPOC-specific spaces will be crucial to combatting the overwhelming whiteness of existing trans initiatives, and they must be viewed as necessary and a priority rather than additional.

Trans people of colour requested more specific and informed support. Amongst the most helpful things would be:

- a hotline – staffed by trained and paid Black trans people and trans people of colour – that can provide general support, signposting to other resources, and crisis support;

- funding for Black trans people – and trans people of colour – specific in-person support spaces, oriented towards young people.

---

2   Key messages adapted from TRANSforming Futures 'Trans people's experiences of healthcare in England' (Hord and Medcalf, 2020b).

TPOC participants:

- 'To get healthcare, someone has to see you as a whole being, if you're white, cis, straight, male, it's easier to see that someone as a whole. When you're anything that deviates from that category, they start nit-picking at everything. You can't be autistic and trans. You can't be queer and have mental illness. These things are pitted against each other. They can't see the complete person.'

- 'Being at university helps – LGBT association, they talk about waiting lists and getting through checklists before starting treatment. But most people are not PoC, can't see a lot of TPOC examples. Could be that I'm not exposed but I did feel a lack. Made me concerned, when it comes to that point, will there be…an additional difficulty.'

- 'Anything to do with gender could be put down to mental illness or autism. It's a risk to be open about many other diagnoses as it could invalidate everything, which has happened before.'

- 'We [trans people of colour] experience gender and the "trans experience" differently, things such as coming out and social stuff are different.'

A study on 'Barriers to health faced by transgender and non-binary black and minority ethnic people' by the Race Equality Foundation (Kattari et al., 2016) also echoed the experience of TPOC in the UK, reiterating the need for more access, more research and more support in general.

- Trans people of colour need improved and more equitable access to health services.

- There is a need for increased access to social services/behavioural health for TPOC communities.

- It should be mandatory for health professionals across all fields to have additional training to support their work with TPOC communities.

- Additional community-based and academic research is needed to examine the experiences of trans people of colour in healthcare.

On faith

When it comes to matters of criminal justice and LGBTQ education in schools, the experiences of Muslim communities cannot be ignored. Faith-based discrimination must be understood on all levels for all people. However, the way religion and whiteness play out in spaces for trans people of colour must be understood too:

> I was raised Muslim, and my faith is something I have struggled with because it's common to hear that you can't identify as queer or trans and be religious, as if it's a contradiction. On top of that, I hear a lot of casual Islamophobia in trans spaces, and it doesn't make me feel safe. I'm already a minority as a person of colour so I feel like if I call it out, I'm becoming a bigger target by identifying as Muslim. I can't truly be myself

and that makes me sad considering I've come this far to be accepted as trans. (Choudrey, 2016)

Religious history, writers and poets are often perceived as one-dimensional, painted as patriarchal. Those who bend spirituality and sexuality are erased from Islamic literature altogether, leaving Western writers as the only source to find LGBTQ solace, furthering connections for LGBTQ people of colour to their faith:

I had grown up to perceive Islam as ascetic and austere, I completely missed an entire genealogy of the faith that directly resonated with me. I had deified the Western literary greats like Oscar Wilde for their queer magic, and completely skipped over the writings of Sufists, like thirteenth-century Persian poet Jalaluddin Rumi, whose dazzlingly spiritual poems are burning with homoerotic desire. It was all there the whole time. Just waiting for me. (Al-Kadhi, 2019, p.280)

Anti-religious views also permeate LGBTQ communities, alienating LGBTQ people of faith who are still fighting to have all of their identities understood and seen. LGBTQ-inclusive places of faith and worship are necessary to provide a space where these communities are safe and accepted, and where all people are welcome too:

I have a gender, it's not male or female, I call it genderqueer, because it's 'just me' otherwise. I have spent a lot of time in the queer community over the last few years and it is really good but I know that a lot of my friends and a lot of others are very anti-faith and anti-religion and sometimes I feel that there

> aren't many people who understand both sides of me; that I'm trans and queer and a Christian at the same time. Luckily, I found a church that is really accepting and they're not only accepting but they encouraged me to express myself. So, I decided to finally get baptised and I invited my whole family. That was really great. (CJ in Twilight People, 2017b)

Sometimes the core aspects of religion can get lost, and for trans people of colour, this is something to return to. For some it is a set of rules to follow and for others it's guidance for a spiritual way of life:

> Hinduism is actually a very tolerant religion… There isn't anything in our scriptures that says, actually, you cannot live your life a certain way, you cannot do this. It's more about love, it's more about compassion. It's more about understanding… The significance of religion, it can be both a blessing and a burden, if I'm completely honest. It can be a blessing in the sense that you get so much from it, but it can also be a burden since people can often feel bogged down by a set of principles that they believe they must live their lives by. (Anjeli in Twilight People, 2017a)

On everything else

The ways our race and gender impact on our lives cannot really be separated from our experiences nor from other parts of our identities. Often the times we are made aware of this unique impact is when we are met with whiteness and cisness: 'Queer and trans people of colour live at the intersections of failure to follow the lines of whiteness, straightness and cisgenderism…

Queerphobia and transphobia within people of colour communities must be understood within the complex histories of coloniality and the coloniality of gender' (Davis, 2017).

Colonization is important to understand if trans people of colour are to be understood too – from stealing and appropriating cultures to whitewashing and the erasure of histories, it sends the message that there is only one way to be trans and that is a Western way:

> I find a lot of the time I feel different to white trans people. When I think about my ethnic background, I feel a great sadness when I think about the trans and queer history I could have had and how it could have shaped my identification, and what colonialism has taken from me. A few of my white trans acquaintances perpetuate the idea that there's 'one way' of thinking about being trans (and that it's a 'civilised' white, Western way with very set language and concepts). But this to me invalidates trans people who exist around the world with different language and concepts to describe their genders. A lot of the time in the UK, trans people of colour are paid lip service and are always an afterthought, despite being a buzzword people like to throw around when talking about inclusion. Even in activist spaces, there's a confusion in how to make real inclusion happen, and that leads to frustration and leaves me with a feeling of emptiness. (Choudrey, 2016)

Our identities are layered. When non-white experiences are viewed through a trans or non-binary lens, another layer of racial stereotypes and cultural insensitivity is added, themes that emerged during a trans and BAME consultation with Stonewall (Beyond the Binary, 2016):

As we transition, we may move between different racial stereotypes – and face different, sometimes threatening responses. We may be hypersexualised as demure Asian women or be perceived as threatening Black men. Our trans identity may add another dimension to racial fetishisation. As non-binary people, we may encounter people appropriating our cultures' identities as historical justification for non-binary identities without being sensitive to the very specific cultural and social context of these identities and the reality of being two-spirit, hijra, third gender or travesti. These identities become rhetorical points rather than lived experiences.

Steffan Zachiyah (2019), a film producer, spoke about his experiences as a Black man of trans experience on brotherhood, meeting Black British trans men, the importance of coming together and being together. The dysphoria falls away and there's more room to be courageous and see parts of themselves:

My gender identity only surfaced when I began to understand the concept of gender roles through culture, religion and social class. Living up to these expectations was always put on a pedestal for me because I believed that the only way for me to be fully accepted was to transition medically, and evolve into the man I always saw myself to be i.e. alpha male, dominant, provider, leader which later displayed itself as bitter, competitive, narcissistic, dogmatic, ignorant and homophobic... The struggles I've faced do not define me, but my story is history for those currently in pain.

There are so many ways non-binary identities are experienced and expressed. It is personal to each non-binary person what that means, and that can also shift over time. Wail Qasim (2016) writer and campaigner, explains: 'For me, being non-binary doesn't mean I have no gender, but that I don't feel I am either a man or a woman. Of course, I was born with a particular body and testosterone has made that body look like that of a man, but these physical characteristics don't sit easily with how I think of myself either. It leads to anguish that many trans people experience, often known as dysphoria.' We also take our friends, family and loved ones on a transition when we come out or change pronouns:

> I recently came out about my gender identity too, asking people to begin referring to me with the pronouns they, them and their instead of he, him and his. My friends have understood and, despite their (unfounded) concerns about the grammatical status of using 'they' in its singular form, they seem to get why I ask them to respect such a request... Like for many of us, who I am seems to be a contradiction, but only because of prejudices unresolved in our society. Learning that we can change those prejudices, rather than forcing ourselves to hide and live with them, saved me from accepting the things that have caused my pain. (Qasim, 2016)

When our identities settle, they can really enrich other parts of ourselves and how we express ourselves. Raju S. Singh, artist, writes in 'Recipes and Rites' (2015, p.169) about their culture, femininity and masculinity coming together and providing solace: 'The more I embraced my Desi culture the more I eased into my identity; it actually made more sense, especially with accepting my femininity alongside the masculinity. Comfort and confident draped around me with my favourite shawls. My protection from the phobic world.'

Trans people of colour must tell our stories for ourselves. Maria Munir (2020), public speaker and human rights defender, spoke with Campaign Bootcamp, expressing the need for consideration to our stories as a commitment – much like inclusivity it is a commitment, not a moment: 'When it comes to the narrative of our story, it becomes important that we're able to tell it ourselves and not constantly be brought up as a strange click-bait video… That suddenly becomes a viral moment and then is never thought about again.'

> Although we have come a long way in educating our organisations, we still have a long way to go. Things are getting better but not enough to make a big impact or a big difference – certainly in my working life. You see communities are now inter-mixing and this will make a difference in the generations to come.
>
> – survey respondent

Section 2

Creating a
Safe(r) Space

Throughout this section you'll see quotes from survey respondents in response to the question, 'What does a trans POC safe space mean to you and what does it look like?' When we create spaces and label them safe(r) we become accountable to those in it. Part of what gives people access to these spaces is trust, says Chloe Cousins, youth and community worker: **'Central to creating safe(r) spaces is establishing trust – trust in those holding the space that they will create an environment where compassion, generosity and accountability is practised. Where this trust isn't present, young people and workers are placed in a really vulnerable position, and that's a huge barrier to feeling able to show up.'**

Nothing is safe, only safer

'Once you designate some spaces as safe, you imply that the

rest are unsafe. It follows that they should be made safer', writes Judith Shulevitz (2015), American journalist and editor. Nothing is safe. Truly, we cannot guarantee a space to be safe – that is to be void of danger, harm or risk of threat. Instead, we do what we can to be accountable to harmdoing and transparent to risk taking. We implement policies or safeguarding procedures to deal with harmful issues and manage risk to make situations safer. Hence, we can only build **safer** spaces – spaces that are safer than the ones we currently exist in. And then we must ask: safer for whom? Safety is subjective to those building a space – are the people building a safe space the same people asking for it or using it? If not, why not? Is this a safe space for everyone who uses it or just those who have built it? There should be evidence, research or a demand for this space by the people it is for. Often research can tell us this without hearing a demand, but much like safety is subjective, as is the researcher with their observations and conclusions.

Dr Stephanie Davis (2017) writes beautifully dere[1] reflections as a QTIPOC 'scholar-activist' before interviewing QTIPOC participants on their experiences of QTIPOC community, groups and safe spaces. Dey share how dere role has shaped the research, parallel to the research impacting dere own journey, but overall being a benefit to enable this research to happen. Whilst reflexivity/positionality statements are familiar to academics, the notion of taking time to consider your position in relation to any community or population should be familiar to all those working with people and communities. Whether

---

[1]   Neopronouns are a new category of neutral pronouns used instead of 'she', 'he' or 'they' when referring to a person, such as dey/dem/dere or ze/zir/zir.

this is explicit or implicit may depend on the circumstances but will influence your intentions and the actions that follow.

It's perhaps obvious to state that the needs of trans people of colour must be included when building a space that will include them, whether it is a TPOC-only space, LGBTQ-only space, BPOC-only space or a community space for all. Whilst it's not always logistically possible for a project to be constructed by the people it is serving, there are other ways that the people it's serving can contribute to the construction. If trans people of colour were not consulted or involved at any of these stages, who is the space really serving and who is the space safe for?

Safety is subjective to those within the group too. What people need to feel empowered and supported is individual, and the solution may not always be a new group or an exclusive group. There's a lot that can be learned from TPOC experiences of the 'safe spaces' that already exist across the UK that raises the question: who is protected from harm and whose safety is prioritized?

Don't they exist already?

A safe space for trans people of colour is more than just stating a space is safe for them. A space is a physical room, a virtual room, the space across face-to-face dialogue or even between message bubbles on a screen. These spaces can and should all be held when we are centring safety. When we designate a space to be safe for trans people of colour, we are implicitly saying that we know what safety means for TPOC, what safety looks like for TPOC and how it feels to be safe as TPOC; we become accountable to their safety. We hold a responsibility in creating spaces to make them safe, and we can certainly try. Even if LGBTQ people are building that safe space, safety is not a one-size-fits-all approach.

Lo Marshall (2016) with UCL Urban Laboratory extensively researched the LGBTQ+ nightlife in London on the current state of safe spaces, capturing TPOC voices about what is missing and what is needed for LGBTQ spaces to be TPOC inclusive. What came out the most was the lack of inclusivity, despite being run by LGBTQ people for LGBTQ people. 'London falls behind many of its global peers when protecting and supporting the queer community, including in failing to provide a dedicated community space', echoed Queer Spaces Network (2018, p.35). Although these comments are reflecting on London nightlife, it's true for many cities in the UK; queer spaces are not protected. LGBTQ communities hold a responsibility to also provide safety for QTIPOC who make up the communities. Victoria Sin (2018, p.27), a visual artist, said, 'Safe spaces, especially for QTIPOC, are vital and missing from the London drag scene and queer community. Queer spaces should take responsibility to amplify and platform the voices of the most marginalized.' And when these spaces are made with QTIPOC communities in mind, the benefits are felt by everyone – 'the most exciting spaces on London's nightlife scene were those that are most inclusive and embraced a queer ethos and community focus' (2018, p.27).

Dr Davis (2017) also found that all groups spoke of the 'whiteness' of LGBTQ communities – these spaces are predominantly made up of white people who dominate the space and the narratives. 'Queerness' and 'transness' are coded in 'white' ways, not only excluding POC but resisting including

QTIPOC and talking about race. The research also noted the importance of QTIPOC groups, that is groups by QTIPOC for QTIPOC, alleviating individual experiences of non-belonging and disconnection and being a place where they can challenge the silences around their histories and discourses that positioned queerness, transness and 'of colourness' as separate. In QTIPOC spaces, these identities can come together.

Safety as a privilege

- Who defines safety?

- How do [we] create systems of safety that centre those who have been most harmed?

- What are non-punitive ways to address and respond to harm?

- How can transformative justice become the way through conflict and harm used by institutions and between individuals?

The Unitarian Universalist Association (n.d.)

To be safe, feel safe and be protected is often a privilege, in that it is available to some and not to all, or that the safety is conditional, dependant on gender expression, conformity or visibility or dependant on perceived or stereotyped racial identities. Safety is a right of all people; unfortunately, it isn't always as objective as this. Conversations around safety are not neutral either. Some of us learn this is the only way to be safe and that the police will protect us, but this is not true for everyone. When our safety is compromised or we are in danger or at harm, we are told to dial '999' and call the emergency services. This is common to read in safeguarding policies – that is, procedures and strategies that protect people from harm. However, involving the emergency services in a harmful situation likely means involving the police. It's crucial that the history and relationship of TPOC communities, in particular Black communities, with the police is understood here.

> To people who care about Black trans men, I want you to know that we are impacted by violence that happens to all Black people. Our lives and experiences do not only (if at all) revolve around being trans. Racism, ableism, poverty, xenophobia, homophobia, criminalization, incarceration, and so many other things impact us – not just one singular issue. Do not take for granted that we sit at the intersections of many kinds of vulnerability. When we lose any Black life, we are affected. And you should defend and fight for all Black lives, which includes our lives too. Black trans women and femmes are the ones who know this best, and we are grateful. (Stephens, 2020)

Where the police do make some feel safe, where the police seem to be the only solution to a problem and even in some organizations where police involvement is part of legal safeguarding duties, this must all be interrogated. What is it that the police do to make some feel safe? What about the communities that do not feel safe and have not been kept safe by the police? What will be implemented to keep these communities safe with or without police involvement?

There are many ways to minimize harm and escalation and protect those already vulnerable within TPOC communities. There are professional advocates to turn to who can liaise with police services to avoid direct contact or communication. For example, in instances of reporting crimes there are ways to do this online or anonymously or through charity advocacy services, where further support for wellbeing is also available. In instances where contact is necessary, consider going to the police station instead of bringing police to the community.

In addition to these alternatives, The Unitarian Universalist Association (n.d.), Sprout Distro (2017) and London Bi Pandas (n.d.), amongst many other organizations, have free educational guides and flowcharts available on the many alternatives on calling the police. These include calling on community, using alternative resources (e.g. for mental health, suicide, fire or medical incidents or sexual or domestic violence where police can potentially escalate or neglect a situation), turning to restorative/transformative justice and taking preventative measures.

Free speech, hate speech and censorship

Safe spaces policies are used to protect guests, members or an organization from threat and hate speech. However, some argue that they can prevent free speech and act as an 'echo chamber', which ultimately causes more harm than good. Some say these policies shield people from subjects and issues that can't be avoided in reality/outside the space, setting up a false idea that they are indeed safe or can be kept safe, or that these policies silence or exclude anyone who doesn't agree with the group beliefs, or those with differing or opposing opinions. The terms 'cancelling', 'no-platforming' or 'censorship' are often used in these discussions. But there is a nuance to be noted, and that is **care**. There is a difference between cancelling/no-platforming/censorship with and without care. Taking action against someone under these imperatives can cause harm if it is not done in the interest of care.

> Safe spaces have been used for good, creating a forum for open discussion about important and emotive topics for women or minorities...but you don't always have to get bogged down in whether 'no platforming' is right or wrong, sometimes the focus is on enjoyment and celebration rather than oppression...at their essence, safe spaces are environments where people can feel confident that they will not be harassed. That their viewpoints will be listened to. Somewhere where you feel comfortable. (Alemoru, 2017)

Why do we need safe spaces and so-called echo chambers in the first place? We navigate many spaces in our lives that are not safe, and the echo chamber may just be one of the places that is safer than the rest. For a trans person of colour, this might be the **only** place they are free from the threat of abuse or harm they face in their daily lives. This place serves a function to imagine a world without transphobia or racism, or at least where measures are taken to prevent these oppressions, where actions are taken with care, where the safety of TPOC is centred and prioritized. Safe spaces held with care serve a function and they need to be protected.

When someone is platformed (either literally, someone who is given a stage, or metaphorically, someone who is allowed to take up space) where the safety of a policy, group or individual is infringed upon, the way this is responded to sends a message about safety and whose safety matters. Whichever decision is made here, it needs to be transparent, and TPOC need to be believed. Question: who does this benefit? Are the decisions made in the interest of TPOC? Again, what does safety mean? For whom?

Nadine Strossen, a law professor, writes in *HATE: Why We Should Resist It with Free Speech, Not Censorship* (2018) about censorship being a last resort, only to be used in an emergency where there is a risk to harm, threats to harm or even where the fear of a threat to harm has been invoked. Strossen particularly stresses censorship as an action where hate and threat are **intentional, incited and imminent**. Free speech can be an effective action against hate speech and an alternative to censorship: more speech, not less. Where this is not the case, seek alternatives, education and open dialogue. There are places where hate speech can be heard, debated and understood just as there are people who are able to lead this work. It should be noted that this work should not be defaulted to the communities it affects. This is where privilege plays a part for these actions done in solidarity and preservation of affected communities.

I suggest that when we move to censoring speech, we question our own intentions too – what is our intention to censor? Can we encourage more speech, not less speech? Are there other alternative actions we can take instead of silencing views that we disagree with? Perhaps there is a conversation that needs to be had with communities who aren't directly affected by what is being said. Can there be more done to combat unconscious bias and ignorance? Call on white people and cis people to lead these unlearnings and use these processes to build solidarity.

Safe spaces as 'a white fantasy'

Continuing on from censorship and upholding safe spaces, Peter James Hudson, professor and historian, writes that the idealized prevention of safety and absence of hate is a fantasy that replicates rather than undoes systems of oppression. This also implies that talking about anti-colonialism, racism, sexism, homophobia and transphobia can be safe, easy and comfortable. Silencing means that intolerance and hate are simply unspoken, and people of colour continue to be harmed by everything that is instead unsaid, whilst the privileged members leave unscathed, nothing undone. Hudson calls this 'a white fantasy' because only someone with racial privilege would assume that this could be a place of safety. Some institutions are already harmful spaces for people of colour where so-called safe spaces are built because issues around race are deemed dangerous. Demanding silence or shaming ignorance will not undo systems of oppression. Hudson (2014, p.6) recalls the history of silencing and racial violence: 'Why is silencing, now, something that protects or enables safety? Who does silence protect and who does silence make safe and who does silence erase? Who has the privilege to demand tolerance?'

Principled spaces as safer spaces

The BARC Collective (Building the Anti-Racist Classroom) have problematized the notion of safe spaces, in that they are not guaranteed. Drawing on conversations with artist and activist Hanalei Ramos, who suggests the use of a 'principled' rather than 'safe' space, BARC suggests that we incorporate guidance and practices (such as a safety officer) that support the creation of appropriate environments for social justice and change (BARC, n.d.). This means working with principles instead of safe space policies, with the idea that we can commit to adhering to a set of principles that guide and shape the space and increase the possibility of safety for all involved.

1. Be aware of your privilege and take a step back so marginalised people can lead, consciously challenging any implicit hierarchy where gender trumps other dimensions of marginalization including race.

2. Believe people's accounts of their experiences of marginalisation, and honour people's vulnerability by not disputing their lived experience, keeping in mind principle number 1.

3. If you feel unsafe for any reason, we have a safety officer with whom you can have a private discussion that will be fed back to organisers anonymously. The organisers commit to taking steps to address any issues and improve the conditions for the rest of the event.

4. All the experiences that are shared here may be deeply personal and should be treated in confidence. While we

cannot guarantee full confidentiality, we request that unless explicit consent is requested and given, that discussions held in the room should stay in the room.

5. We encourage participants to tweet, make posts, comments and critiques using the hashtag #barcworkshop, but to respect other participants, you are not permitted to make derogatory comments or posts about any person in the room, or to share experiences that are not yours without explicit consent.

6. While these principles are intended to apply to all, they are written in recognition of existing power structures that continue to marginalise people of colour, perpetuate anti-Blackness and promote white privilege/power. This should be kept in mind throughout the workshop.

Our Principles from the BARC Collective (BARC, n.d.)[2]

Safe spaces as 'X only'

Whilst some spaces require the exclusion of certain people to enable the spaces to be inclusive, the intentions behind policies that state 'women only' or 'no cis men' must be interrogated. This is particularly seen in, but not limited to, places of worship, feminist communities and groups organizing around women's rights. Statements like this must be unpicked in the

---

2   Free community resources from the BARC Collective can be found on their website: https://barcworkshop.org/resources.

same ways safety is: who is defining safety? Who is being included in this? Who is really being protected?

'Women only'

'Women only' has been historically used to protect spaces for women without men present. There is nothing wrong with having gender-segregated spaces when they serve a purpose to protect those within them. However, when put into practice, this implicitly means 'cis women only' and is used to exclude trans women and trans-feminine people on the false basis that they are not women. This harmful action gives permission for gender/body policing and the violence of transmisogyny (see Section 3) that it is rooted in. There is nothing feminist about this. Trans women and trans-feminine people are not protected.

> I must remind them that it is never feminist when some women are silenced and sacrificed to make room for the more privileged women. (Koyama, 2006, p.703)

One of the reasons given is that trans women and trans-feminine people have male privilege or still have a 'maleness' about them from their history as boys/men or from being raised with male privilege. Trans women and trans-feminine people have never been boys or men or experienced the world as cis men, and therefore have never benefited from male privilege; the patriarchy does not serve or empower them.

Another reason for excluding trans people is due to any biology/genitalia that trans women and trans-feminine people are assumed to have and may have. Not only does this objectify trans women and trans-feminine people; it also reduces their identity to their genitals and implies that boys/men are more powerful or dangerous on the basis of their penis, genitals, hormones, size, etc.

> at its core, feminism is based on the conviction that women are far more than the sex of the bodies that we are born into, and our identities and abilities are capable of transcending the restrictive nature of the gender socialisation we endure during our childhoods. I have yet to meet the person who can explain to me how refusing trans women the right to participate in women's spaces and events is consistent with this most central tenet of feminism. (Serano, 2007, pp.238–239)

Sisters Uncut, a feminist direct action group, meets in spaces that are not open to men. In the past they have organized in mixed settings before; however, women's voices were not heard and their needs were not met. They found this to be a drain on energy, a block to action and counterproductive. As part of their safe spaces policy, they have a gender inclusion policy that revises 'women only' rules into a policy that empowers trans people to join, validating their right to their gender, identity and safety.

> Our meetings should be inclusive and supportive spaces for all women (trans, intersex and cis) and all nonbinary, agender and gender variant people. Self-definition is at the sole discretion of that individual. We do not police gender in our spaces. If you are here it is because you feel that you are included by our gender inclusion policy, and therefore you are welcome. Our meetings and spaces are not open to people who identify solely or primarily as men. If you have any

> queries regarding our gender inclusion policy, please don't
> hesitate to ask questions. (Sisters Uncut, 2018)

'No cis men'

The intention behind this rule, often seen at LGBTQ events, club
nights and activist spaces, was to counter gendered violence
and gender-based oppression and to have spaces away from
the cis male gaze. However, the impact alienates trans men,
trans women and many non-binary people instead.

It gives permission to fetishize trans men and trans-
masculine people, which often happens at the gaze/hands of
cis LGBQ women. Again, it is reductive and objectifies trans
people's genitals. The hidden implication is not only that trans
men's genitals are different from cis men's genitals, but that
these genitals make trans men different from cis men, i.e. not
men. It means that trans men need to out themselves or look
visibly trans, to risk being not safe, not believed. What's not
being said explicitly is that this rule means no one with penises, and that safety is assigned to genitals and gender assigned
at birth. Trans men are often grouped with cis women, and
trans women are not often considered (read: excluded). This
also gives permission for the violence of gender/body policing,
which will negatively impact trans women and trans-feminine
people the most. This kind of statement is also used as a
dating preference, seen on dating profiles carrying the same
level of harm:

> 'I date women and trans men' is the definition of cissexism.
> It's basing your frame for sexuality on the gender coercively
> assigned to a person by their doctor at birth, not on that

> person's actual identity. In this case, we're talking about folks who were assigned female. Of course, 'women' means cis women – trans women totally drop off the map. (Truitt, 2012)

CN Lester (2011) also writes about the 'no cis men' rule when it comes to dating and community spaces and the fixation on genitals being an unjust reason to include or exclude a trans man. Serano (2013) describes this as 'FAAB mentality', where 'FAAB' means 'female assigned at birth', appropriated by many cis LGBQ women who wish to convey their affiliation with trans men and to distance themselves from trans women as well as cis men. Our preferences and policies are not neutral, nor do they always protect trans people or benefit feminist and activist movements. If any rule of exclusion is to be used, it needs to be explicit what is really being said and why it's being used.

'TPOC only'

For trans people of colour, there is a power in having spaces only for trans people of colour. This is a decision that should come from people of colour themselves – we should have autonomy over the group membership if it is to centre us and TPOC communities.

> Good practice is the ability for TPOC to self-determine whether a space can be exclusively for TPOC/POC.
>
> – survey respondent

We must understand what safety means, feels and looks like for TPOC in order to understand why TPOC-only spaces are necessary. 'QTPOC groups create spaces of affirmation and recognition as participants describe feeling queerly raced, in which they recognize shared and collective experiences of negation. This provides the potential for developing critical, decolonising consciousness and creatively and reparatively re-imagining a past, present and future of representation and inclusion', Dr Stephanie Davis (2017, p.190) writes in dere research on QTIPOC experiences in the UK. Dr Davis found that organizing and attending QTIPOC spaces combatted isola-tion and built a sense of belonging, provided an antidote to the disconnection and created an alternative space for their bodies that are disoriented from the wider world too. Participants found a sense of confidence, security, connection, community and comfort in shared experiences and shared aspects of iden-tity with other trans people of colour. 'For QTPOC then the sharing of cultural expression may support connection across ethnic differences, while acknowledging the relations between people of colour communities and cultural expression in a city like London. The joy and experience of connection challeng-es the feelings of not belonging, creating feelings of being affirmed, and also feelings of "home"' (Davis, 2017, p.190).

In addition to this, TPOC-only spaces provide motivation and empowerment. The white gaze and cis gaze are absent from a space, alleviating any risks of harm or difficulties that come with unchecked privileges. Energy and time diverted by educating white people or mediating racial prejudice can be focused on building the TPOC community.

There is more to establishing an empowering TPOC-only safe space than simply excluding cis white people, as racism, anti-Blackness and gender oppression still operate – this is explored in Section 3.

More than just toilets

Discussion around safe spaces and inclusion of trans people quickly falls into a discussion about bathroom facilities: men's toilets, women's toilets and the few accessible toilets, which are often the only gender-neutral toilets. Whilst it is important to have appropriate facilities, the conversation on trans inclusion gets lost when we focus only on toilets. When we reduce trans inclusion to just toilets, we reduce the needs of trans people to just one need.

'The intense focus on the policing of gender in toilet spaces distracts us from thinking about how the space outside toilets is equally rigidly gendered and policed', says Dr Francis White (2020), a senior lecturer. They have explored 150 years of the use of public toilets and the cultural anxieties about social change that play out in them and how debates about who belongs in them comes into the discussion.

Until I came out as trans, I never thought this much about toilets. But when you consider the following list, you can see it is about much more than just toilets:

- Is there only one gender-neutral toilet in the whole building?

- Is it on the very top floor or in a dark basement – basically, is it really far away?

- Is it an accessible toilet? Can trans people with disabilities use it?

- Is the only accessible toilet a gender-neutral toilet? Are you expecting all disabled and non-binary people to use one toilet in the whole building?

- Are staff telling others which toilet people should go to, choosing their gender for them ('The toilet? Yes, the men's is just there on the left.')?

- Are trans people going to be safe to use whatever toilet they want? Will they be questioned on their bathroom choices?

- Are trans women in particular going to be safe in the women's toilet; to use the toilet they want?

- Do the staff understand gender diversity, the importance of trans and non-binary inclusion and why these gender-neutral toilets exist?

- When you hire external venues or go out for staff events, are you making sure there are gender-neutral and accessible toilet facilities?

- Are you thinking about trans people accessing spaces outside the building?

- Are you complaining to these venues when the toilet facilities are limited, therefore restricting who in your team can come and excluding your staff?

- And are you apologizing to trans people when you hire that venue anyway?

- Is the complaints system designed to hear and record incidents as transphobic and not just discrimination, disagreement or a distasteful joke? Let's call it what it is: transphobia.

- Are there visible trans allies and supporters in the institution who can advocate for trans staff and guests so it isn't just the responsibility of trans people and there isn't the expectation that we will speak out for ourselves? We are often too occupied with healing from the effects of institutional and everyday oppression to actually be able to fight it.

Jen Slater and Charlotte Jones (2020) have researched what makes a safe and accessible toilet space, including recommendations, example signage and toilet design toolkits.

EXAMPLE SIGNAGE FOR ALL-GENDER TOILETS

Sign One:

Toilet

This toilet can be used by people of any gender.

Men's and women's toilets are available at [insert location of closest men's and women's toilets, if available]. An all-gender accessible toilet is available at [insert location of closest accessible toilet]. Changing Places Toilets are available at [insert location of closest Changing Places Toilets].

Sign Two (similar wording could also be used, for example, to email staff in a workplace):

All-gender Toilets

What is an all-gender toilet?
An all-gender toilet is a toilet that anybody can use, regardless of their gender.

Why have you installed all-gender toilets?
As an organisation committed to equality and diversity, providing an all-gender toilet is important.

All-gender toilets are useful for a range of people and situations including, parents with children of a different gender; those who care for people of a different gender; some disabled people who have a personal assistant of a different gender; and some people whose gender is questioned in the toilet including some trans and non-binary people.

For some people, not having access to an all-gender toilet prevents them from leaving the house or leads to them reducing what they eat and drink in order to avoid using the toilet.

Do you have men's and women's toilets?
The closet men's and women's toilets are also available at [insert locations].

(Slater and Jones, 2020)

Societal and cultural expectations don't just dictate who should or shouldn't be in certain toilets, but also implicitly dictate how people should and shouldn't behave in men's and women's toilets. It is not just gender that is policed: 'There were also racialised aspects to assumptions of "appropriate" use. One Muslim father described the suspicion aroused when washing his son in the communal sink area, in order to perform ablution. Whilst this points to the importance of providing facilities for ablution, it also highlights the need to challenge racist and Islamophobic perceptions beyond the toilet... Religious beliefs are often used as a justification for the unsuitability of all-gender toilets, and their potential to offend or exclude. Through our research, this concern has usually been raised by people who do not discuss their own experiences of faith. Rather, they use their own perceptions about other religious people, often of Islamic faith, to dismiss the idea of all-gender toilet provision.'

Whether it is a new gender-neutral toilet or de-gendering existing bathroom facilities, all-gender toilets benefit everyone in a range of situations: parents/carers with children of a different gender, some disabled people who have a personal assistant of a different gender and anyone whose gender is questioned in the toilet. Putting on a new sign shouldn't be the end point in making bathroom facilities inclusive of trans people; gendered assumptions must be challenged (e.g. sanitary bins in toilets for all genders) and consideration that whilst these signs can increase a sense of safety for trans people, this must be explained sensitively.

Creating an accessible space

'At the intersection of being trans and disabled is grief. We are in a constant state of grief for our past selves, as well as a state of trepidation for the future. As for the present, we are just trying to constantly adapt to our situations, manage the expectations of others, and ultimately, survive', says activist Noorulann Shahid (2020). The experiences of trans people with disabilities must be heard, seen and believed. We must understand that those with in/visible disabilities, health conditions and impairments are a part of our communities. When we don't acknowledge this, we fail people with disabilities, and we fail our communities as a whole. When we create spaces for trans people of colour, we must ensure we are making safe and accessible spaces for trans people of colour with disabilities.

Before we can make a space accessible, we must understand ableism. Author Talila 'TL' Lewis (2021) has come up with a working definition of ableism:

> A system that places value on people's bodies and minds based on societally constructed ideas of normality, intelligence, excellence, desirability, and productivity. These constructed ideas are deeply rooted in anti-Blackness, eugenics, misogyny, colonialism, imperialism and capitalism. This form of systemic oppression leads to people and society determining who is valuable and worthy based on a person's language, appearance, religion and/or their ability to satisfactorily [re]produce, excel and 'behave'.

Lewis adds that that ableism is experienced by everyone – you don't have to be disabled to experience it. We all internalize ableism and we all navigate the systems and institutions that are ableist. It is the responsibility of able-bodied people to challenge able-bodied privilege, value lived experiences of people with disabilities and make spaces accessible.

Artist Raju Rage (2020) says, 'The problem is that the people who are excluded are absent in the first instance.' When building a space for a community, the people who it is for must be present. Often people are asked about their access needs or requirements when attending events, but why wait? Ask about access needs beforehand, such as when organizing an event, so they are implemented in the structure and delivery itself instead of something that has to be accommodated within an inaccessible event. Accessibility is not an afterthought. People with disabilities are not an afterthought – they are a part of the community and need to be thought of first. Ask about access needs beforehand, such as when building a safe space, and include people with disabilities so that 'safety' itself includes accessibility. Engaging in disability justice and anti-ableist practice is a choice. Make conscious choices and internalize accessibility as an intention.

Rage speaks about 'access intimacy', that is to do more than simply accommodate other people but to change the ableist and exclusionary systems and spaces we navigate – to actually care about accessibility enough to do something about it. This is a practice introduced by Mia Mingus, writer and trainer, in her essay titled 'Access intimacy: the missing link' (2011):

> Access intimacy is not charity, resentfulness enacted, intimidation, a humiliating trade for survival or an ego boost. In fact, all of this threatens and kills access intimacy. There is a good feeling after and while you are experiencing access intimacy.

> It is a freeing, light, loving feeling. It brings the people who are a part of it closer; it builds and deepens connection. Sometimes access intimacy doesn't even mean that everything is 100% accessible. Sometimes it looks like both of you trying to create access as hard as you can with no avail in an ableist world. Sometimes it is someone just sitting and holding your hand while you both stare back at an inaccessible world.

Rage hopes for care and compassion to be written into policy, to support disabled artists and creatives, and acknowledges that this won't happen in institutions that are innately structed around hierarchies. Accessibility ultimately benefits everybody, as does inclusivity. There are many things that can be done to make spaces accessible, but they largely depend on asking people with disabilities who are using the space what they need in addition to asking the able-bodied people what can they do. Gabe Moses, writer for disability justice, has a list about how to make your social justice space accessible to people with disabilities as a good starting point.

1. Make Sure Everyone Can Get in the Door

2. Make Sure the Message is Reaching Everyone

3. Make Sure Everyone's Message Can Reach Others

4. Don't Stigmatize Non-Normative Behavior

5. Avoid Language that Further Marginalizes Disabled People

6. Understand That We Are as Diverse as Any Other Group of People

7. Let Disabled People Speak for Ourselves and Determine How Best to Serve Our Own Needs

(Moses, 2019)

There are many free guides available depending on your individual situation. Seeds for Change (n.d.) have a guide on choosing and preparing venues to meet everyone's access requirements. Diversity and Ability (n.d.) have free resources to improve accessibility online, on your website and on your social media platforms plus links to assistive technology, software and apps. Zoom (n.d.) and Microsoft (n.d.) teams both have comprehensive guides on ensuring your online events and workplaces can be accessible too. And if you can't (or won't) implement accessibility across your organization or community spaces, be ready to respond and explain why.

A TPOC safe(r) space

When asked what a trans POC safe space looks like, participants from my anonymous survey responded with themes around flexibility, confidentiality, comfort, belonging and being affirmed, listened to, seen and heard in their fullness.

Confidentiality

> **"** Somewhere that there is confidentiality and I am sur-
> rounded by like-minded people and able to connect with
> people my age. **"**
>
> – survey respondent

Confidentiality as a term means that what is spoken is private or secret; however, it calls to be unpicked. What confidentiality means to most professionals is that what is spoken about between parties is kept between those parties unless there is a risk of harm to the person involved or anyone else. There are other instances where confidentiality can be broken; however, this must always be discussed with the person involved wherever possible. These are opportunities for transparency. What does confidentiality mean for your organization? How is confidentiality explained? Can it be explained in simple, accessible language? Does the group trust in those running it? What are the instances where confidentiality is broken? Is there a risk that racial bias will play a part where certain people are seen as harmful or a threat? How will this be navigated? How confidentiality is spoken about will indicate what safety means for an organization and how the safety of TPOC will be protected.

Listening

> **"** I want spaces where BAME/POC trans folx's voices are
> actually boosted/listened to, and if the community/page/
> space does something problematic accidentally, they're

willing to take responsibility and do better, instead of getting defensive or dismissing it. Including in the comments!! It's not enough to post inclusive content – you've got to create a safe community, which means making sure your readers have a safe space to have discussions. That means blocking trolls/harassers and racist/transantagonistic/ableist accounts so that they can't comment on your posts and/or hurt your readers.

– survey respondent

Where possible, platform TPOC voices and create channels for dialogues to take place. Is there a way for attendees or members to feed back about what the space was like and suggest improvements; does everyone know that they can speak and who to speak to? Is there anyone to speak to who is TPOC, or are there others who can act as trusted people? And when TPOC are speaking, practice active listening and 'radical listening'. Understand that radical listening is not a sacrifice but an act of love, it isn't waiting for your turn to speak, as Hempstock and Andry (2017) write. It empowers you and others through sharing experiences and creates connection and commonalities.

When we talk, we take up space – perhaps our privileges enable us to do so, thus we have the potential to dominate a space and disempower others from speaking. To prevent this, some use the guideline 'take space, make space': we should be aware of when we are taking space, be mindful of the privileges that enable us to speak or speak over others and then create space for others by letting others speak instead of us, or simply by listening.

> A space not dominated by white people, where people's genders and pronouns are respected. I don't know if I feel that a majority white space can be a POC safe space, even if people's intentions are good. Too many white people make an environment feel like you're on show or even well-intentioned people often lead to an environment where it feels like you have to speak up if you're black just because there's such an imbalance, rather than allowing people who actually want to say something to speak. A space which is less draining is one which is a safe space, one where you feel energised rather than tired.

– survey respondent

Flexibility

> Constantly able to change. What works for one does not work for all, so there can't be one 'safe space' for everyone. Right now this space would be closed to those who do not self-identity [as TPOC], but often I have wanted to feel welcome & protected by my cis friends. A trans safe space is a place without conflict, but this doesn't even happen when spaces are all-trans (see: truscum), and in inter-racial communities! I guess it would be safe if everyone was willing to continue to grow and educate themselves.

– survey respondent

Will a safe space be governed by an organizational policy, guidelines or a contract? How will it be interacted with? These words carry different understandings and offer different flexibilities. Flexibility also means accessibility – flexibility is an access need too. Whether it is a safe space, accessibility or conflict agreement policy, does everyone (staff, members, guests) have to agree to it? Is this a working or fixed agreement? When and how does the agreement get adapted? For some, it is introduced and rewritten with contributions from everyone at the start of every group; for others, it is given at the start of a meeting or sent out ahead of time. Consider the people who are absent and how they could input to these agreements in an accessible way. Lastly, how do we know when they are working? Measuring and feedback processes must be designed and implemented to ensure that the agreement is still working for the group – and when it's not working, accountability processes must also be created or implemented too.

Belonging

There are many ways to feel like you belong. Being included, visible and represented are all ways we know we belong somewhere.

> When there are other people there like me. It's hard being the only one in a space, I feel awkward. It should be comfortable, good lighting, music and a lot of snacks.
>
> – survey respondent

> I wish there were more places like cafes for LGBT people rather than just clubs and somewhere that I can go during the day since my family don't let me go out late.
>
> – survey respondent

Belonging can be as simple as making people feel welcome and cared for. Consider accessibility again; what good lighting looks like, what food people can and can't have. Asking about light, noise and chemical and food sensitivity and allergies *and* following through with this is one way to demonstrate solidarity; this is basic inclusion. Consider the types of events and timings of events being run and how they can exclude young people and people with caring responsibilities, dependants or children, for example. There are some general understandings around timings of work/school hours depending on who the event is aimed at, to be mindful of school and religious holidays, or whether a creche or financial support for caring could be offered; however, it's always best to ask what could enable people to be included. Both the event and the experience should be accessible to TPOC.

> Being included, being given space to share and contribute, being able to speak about things which may be specific to race and being received without defensiveness.
>
> – survey respondent

> Having a fully supported network of people that share the same issues/experiences as oneself.
>
> – survey respondent

How are TPOC brought into conversations and decisions? If it is a space for TPOC, make sure TPOC are visible and included, whether there are TPOC staff or volunteers, or TPOC are visible in the conversations or activities that are happening – speak about TPOC celebrities, role models and histories. Make TPOC visible in a room or virtual room by sharing TPOC resources or videos/audio that is by TPOC too. Where are TPOC represented in the organization or community? TPOC are often in the front-facing roles as frontline staff or volunteers working directly with people. What can be done to show that TPOC belong in leadership too? Representation matters on all levels.

D/E/A/T/H D/R/O/P

This is for all those that occupy the space between fabulous and fear.
Between fierceness and ferocious.
Between the finger snap and a punch.
Between the death drop and death.
Between the fierce and the faggot.
Between the faggot and fag.
I wonder if the same people who harass us in the street, are the same ones asking us for lipstick in the club.
The same people who go to the drag race viewing party, only to ignore us in danger the next morning.
The same guy that danced the bar with me last Monday will inevitably kick me out the bathroom on Tuesday.
When they say 'yaas God' are they praying to be forgiven for the abuse they threw?
How does jealousy manifest on the dance floor?
This is for all those that keep the party going, but are never asked how they are getting home.
For all those that navigate a body in limbo between the death and the drop.
To be the life of the party but always still left behind.
To be in everyone's photo's but in no one's thoughts.
I wonder who gets to death drop without the fear of dropping

dead?
Will you pay for my Uber ride home, my friend?
Or did you not realise I could talk.

Travis Alabanza (2017)

Section 3

Holding a Safe(r) Space

We have to actively build safe spaces for trans people of colour and welcome them in. **'As trans people of colour, we often believe we aren't worthy of taking up space. We're repeatedly told we're too proud, too loud, too alive. Spaces aren't created for us. We must bust them open with primal screams and clenched fists,'** writes creator Radam Ridwan (2020). Once our experiences are heard and it's understood that it still may not be enough and be wrong and be destroyed, only then will a space be useful for us. Spaces must respond and continue to respond to trans people of colour.

Intersectionality, again

As much as I personally refrain from saying it again and again, it bears repeating: intersectionality. Speak about it when you are not hearing it spoken about. Think about it when you are not reading it written. It's wrong to think that once we've thought about intersectionality at one stage, we don't have to think about it again. Intersectionality is a process, not a one-time event. Every time we are thinking about people and community, we need to be thinking intersectionality and asking ourselves: what identities and experiences do these people have; which people are a part of this community; who are they? The people on the margins, excluded and forgotten, are often the people on the intersections. We need to include everyone.

Solidarity needs to exist within these communities as well as between them. Think about race and all the intersections within and around gender – apply a Black or POC lens to gender, masculinity and femininity. Consider class and how it is woven through culture, language, access, dis/ability – do not forget these intersections.

Understanding racism, gender diversity or class alone does not happen without understanding the other intersections. You cannot pick a single oppression whilst ignoring another or without knowing the rest. The following sections are divided as a starting point to understanding racism, gender diversity and class; these are by no means divided issues. The further these issues are explored the more crossovers there will be.

"Only in the last 1–2 years has it been easier to find online resources that aren't cissexist or overwhelmingly white. Every time you find a website/online community you think is a safe space, you find out the hard way that it's queer-friendly **but** acephobic, or it's trans-friendly **but** ableist...if that makes sense? Most of the non-binary groups I tried joining on Facebook don't post trigger warnings for content with trans-antagonism or ableism (they're also overwhelmingly white, but no surprise there).

– survey respondent

Understanding racism

I mentioned white supremacy in Section 1. Understanding racism starts with understanding white privilege, as this is where the power is. The roots of white privilege are white supremacy. This is important because not only is it a part of history – white supremacy has been a part of nationalism and mainstream ideologies for centuries – but also it has taught white people how to be in this position of power and to take it up. In order to justify this as a dominant status, whiteness was taught and represented as stronger, smarter or better through so-called science and biological research – which were of course led by white people. Dominance, intelligence or 'goodness' based on race is incorrect. Such asserting research is not neutral; it mirrors the lens it sees through.

Today, white supremacy is designed not to be seen or questioned. A function of systems of oppression is to be confusing – it means we are less able to figure out what's actually happening and therefore less likely to challenge it, and we all partake in it. This is due to unconscious conditioning, so that even when we understand racism is wrong at face value, we're conditioned to still believe the whiteness is justified as the dominant or default; we don't see how often we associate white culture and experiences with what is 'good'. This is evidenced through racial microaggressions, colourism (the favouritism of lighter skin over darker skin) and anti-Blackness. People of colour and white people are all subject to this unconscious conditioning because, for the most part, we are all socialized under the system of white supremacy, historically and globally. However, white people in the dominant position must do more to respond to a system they are benefiting from and are a part of, especially when it is brought to their attention – in particular, when white people are called racist. There are some common reactions, including tension and discomfort – it's all part of the unconditioning and unlearning process.

Dr Kathy Obear (n.d.), author and social justice facilitator, has designed a resource for white people to name and interrupt racist responses and attitudes – specifically those that don't lead to a change in behaviour or awareness. Below is a sample of twelve statements for white people to read. Similar to the privilege exercises, before you read this list, please make sure you have a space to reflect afterwards, either by yourself or by speaking with another white person. Obear also has resources to support dialogue and conversation amongst white people and allies. Take your time, find a paper or document to write on, scribble, type, draw, react however you want and be as honest as you can.

Either consciously or unconsciously, do you:

1. Believe that I and other whites have 'earned' what we have, rather than acknowledge the extensive white privilege and unearned advantages we receive

2. Want people of color to conform and assimilate to white cultural norms and practices

3. Defensively focus on my 'good intent' and lack of malice rather than on the negative racist impact of my behaviours

4. Focus on how much progress we have made as a society or organisation, rather than on how much more needs to change to truly create equity and racial justice

5. Want people of color to 'get over it' and move on quickly, stop talking about race and racism

6. 'Walk on eggshells' and act more distant and formal with people of colour than I do with whites

7. Exaggerate the level of intimacy I have with individual people of colour

8. Fear I will be seen and 'found out' as racist, having racial prejudice

9. Dismiss the racist experiences of people of color with comments such as: 'That happens to me too... You're too sensitive... That happened because of [blank] and has nothing to do with race!'

10. Compete with other whites to be 'the good white': the best ally, the most socially just one, the one people of color let into their circle, etc.

11. Seek and demand, approval, validation and recognition from people of color

12. Disengage if I feel any anxiety or discomfort in discussions about race and racism

Obear (n.d.)

REFLECT ON

- What dynamics have you observed or witnessed?
- Which dynamics have you personally participated in?
- Which statement made you think most?

To reiterate, this is simply to name and acknowledge common behaviours of white people: fear, defensiveness, shutting down and stepping back. You may have also heard of things like white guilt, white shame and white fragility, which might be coming up for you now as you read this. This list is here is for educational and accountability purposes. You can implicate, question and change yourself and other white people; you can act differently and take the risk of being wrong. This is all a part of understanding and unlearning racism.

Racism is more than just a slur or offensive thought; racism is a system: it is prejudice plus power, that is, racial prejudice and the institutional social power to enforce it. White people hold that institutional power because of white supremacy and white colonial history. Saying this, 'reverse racism' doesn't exist. People of colour do not have a colonial history nor do they have a history of oppressing white people. People of colour can show prejudice against white people – it is equally condemnable as prejudice against anyone for their race – but this form of discrimination does not come with institutional or systemic privilege. It is not racism, the reverse of racism nor as insidious a form of oppression as per this definition.

Understanding racism continues by seeing race. 'Not seeing race does little to deconstruct racist structures or materially improve the conditions which people of colour are subject to daily. In order to dismantle unjust, racist structures, we must see race. We must see who benefits from their race, who is disproportionately impacted by negative stereotypes about their race, and to who power and privilege is bestowed upon – earned or not – because of their race, their class, and their gender. Seeing race is essential to changing the system,' writes Reni Eddo-Lodge (2018a, p.84).

Understanding racism continues by understanding the specific harms faced by Black people: anti-Blackness or anti-Black racism. This is perpetuated not only by white people but non-Black people of colour too. 'It's important that as non-black people of colour, we learn, quickly, to frame ourselves not just as oppressed people but as oppressors too. We need to separate our experiences of racism and our trauma from that of black people's, which is unique', writes Aisha Mirza (2020). The proof of anti-Blackness is in our past; the UK is responsible for the slave trade, colonialism and imperialism, and today Black representation is missing in UK decision-making positions. Terms like BAME are used to merge Black experiences with non-Black people of colour, Cephas Williams (2020) warns, writing about the UK as complicit in anti-Black racism and the responsibility to fight it.

Anti-Blackness must be recognized within East Asian, South Asian and all non-Black communities, from perpetu-ating colourism; sharing videos of Black people dying; carica-turing/parodying Black people in TV, film, art and gifs; using

African American Vernacular English (AAVE) or accents; and erasing Black people in LGBTQ culture by not learning about the history of drag and voguing in predominantly Black roots in New York (see *Yes Magazine* (2020) for more on unlearning anti-Blackness; Daikon (2018) and Michelle Kim (2020) for anti-Blackness in East Asian communities; South Asians for Black Lives (2020) and Tamima Begum (2020) for anti-Blackness in South Asian communities).

Some of what is described above are called microaggressions. Microaggressions are small, subtle gestures, phrases and behaviours that are easily overlooked or sometimes integrated as part of mainstream culture. Receiving these once or twice will not feel like much; however, over time, these build up and it becomes heavy. They may not be understood by the person doing them, nor the person receiving them, but the emotional and sometimes physical impact is the same as the oppression faced on larger more overt levels.

Sue et al. (2007) studied examples of racial microaggressions, what themes they came under and the message these comments send.

'**Where are you from?**' When people of colour are assumed to be born in another country, the message is that they are not British or English.

'**When I look at you, I don't see colour.**' When people do not want to acknowledge race, they assimilate to the dominant culture, denying people of colour's experiences and POC identities.

'**I'm not a racist; I have several Black friends.**' When white people deny their racial biases, they're saying they are immune to racism because of the people of colour they are surrounded by in a personal capacity.

Other examples are behaviours, such as security or store clerks following customers of colour around a store or white people checking their valuables as a person of colour passes, implying criminality based on their race. Another example is people of colour being ignored at a store counter and a white person behind them getting served. When a white person is given preferential treatment, the message is that people of colour are less valued customers.

Cultural appropriation is another way microaggressions are emulated, that is, appropriating, stealing or exploiting parts of other people's cultures, heritages or faiths as a costume, an aesthetic or an accessory in a way that is insensitive and offensive. Halloween is a popular time of year to dress up; however, culture is not a costume or caricature. There are many ways to appreciate cultures without further stigmatizing people of colour or perpetuating harmful stereotypes. Jarune Uwujaren, writer, draws the link between privilege and cultural appropriation, where it demonstrates the imbalance of power that still exists between cultures that have been colonized and the ex-colonizers. Uwujaren writes about cultural exchange as best practice, 'engaging with a culture as a respectful and humble guest, invitation only' (2013).

Notice all the ways racism shows up in your spaces. Acknowledge it in a way that is safe for the group or the individual and name it for what it is. When we do, we believe Black people and people of colour; we value them by keeping spaces safe for them.

Understanding gender diversity

Trans inclusion is more than just understanding trans identities; it is understanding the full range of gender diversity.
This enables everyone to position themselves within gender
systems – gender oppression is not just a trans problem. Gender liberation benefits everyone.

> People do not understand gender non-conforming people.
> There is not enough knowledge or public archives about the
> fact that we exist. People think our liberation starts and stops
> at getting our pronouns right. Or that we are 'in the middle' of
> a further stage. That we are a phase until we realise we are
> actually man or actually women. We are never seen as real-
> ised. As full. As complete. I think people need to understand
> that if we liberate gender non-conforming feminine people,
> we will liberate us all. (Alabanza 2017)

The gender binary – meaning the two genders, man and woman
– operates within systems to restrict the roles, expectations and
expressions of men and women. Biphobia and homophobia
both police gender expression, sexuality based on gender-based
attraction and masculinity and femininity. These forms of
oppression revolve around how we view women and femininity
as inferior, which is rooted in sexism. Transphobia dictates and
upholds binary genders, cissexism, that trans men and trans
woman are somehow less than cis men and cis women. The idea
that certain genitalia are more at fault for patriarchy or violence
is a dangerous one that perpetuates more cissexism than safety.
It also harms trans women, regardless of how we ideate or
use our bodies, and it creates an exclusion that we may feel

targeted by even if the sign says "trans women are welcome,"' writes Brook Shelley (2016), who continues to explain that the idea that 'penises' should be excluded is a call back to outdated second-wave feminist ideas that all violence is male violence.

> While violence may be statistically higher in 'men', it isn't necessarily limited to cis men, and may implicate masculinity more than assigned gender. The belief that queer relationship violence, or lesbian- or woman-perpetuated violence, doesn't exist or is incredibly rare is the kind of gaslighting that can keep a partner or girlfriend of an abuser from seeking help or escaping a dangerous or abusive relationship. We can only truly limit abuse in spaces by watching for abusive behaviour and having zero tolerance for it, without an eye towards how the person enacting it may appear or present to others.

Trans women, trans-feminine people and transmisogyny

Being aware of the gender binary means being aware of different genders and the different systems that operate to enforce it – in particular sexism, misogyny and transmisogyny. We know this because the systems that are agitated by the breaking of gender norms and blurring of gender roles are the same ones that uphold the patriarchy and male-centred gender hierarchy that exists in our society, as Julia Serano addresses in her Trans Woman Manifesto (2007), calling for the end of the scapegoating, deriding and dehumanizing of trans women everywhere. When the majority of anti-trans discrimination, ridicule, exclusion and violence is against trans women and trans-feminine people, it is not transphobia, it is transmisogyny – we must call it what it is. This specific form of discrimination against trans people expressing femaleness or femininity and not just crossing gender boundaries is transmisogyny.

Serano explains that anti-trans discrimination is steeped in traditional sexism; it's not enough to simply challenge binary gender norms (i.e. oppositional sexism) and we must also challenge the idea that femininity is inferior to masculinity: 'By necessity, trans activism must be at its core a feminist movement.'

> It is only when we move away from the idea that there are 'opposite' sexes, and let go of the culturally-derived values that are assigned to expressions of femininity and masculinity, that we may finally approach gender equity. By challenging both oppositional and traditional sexism simultaneously, we can make the world safe for those of us who are queer, those of us who are feminine, and for those of us who are female, while simultaneously empowering people of all sexualities and genders. (Serano 2007)

Non-binary people and inclusivity

There is so much beauty in gender diversity and gender fluidity. Trans people have existed for longer than hormone blockers and medical intervention – trans people's identities are about more than medical transition. Our identities and expressions are beyond. Non-binary people are navigating a binary world that excludes them daily. There are so many choices we make based on our gender and we have so many choices made for us based on our perceived gender.

Non-binary people's genders are not recognized for the most part. Some changes are happening slowly to introduce more gender options on forms and more title options on applications. For example the UK 2021 census included an option for non-binary genders for the first time. However, safety, protection and recognition for non-binary people depends on more than an 'Mx' title or 'x' gender marker; it depends on a change in attitudes too and solidarity from the cis and binary trans communities.

Challenge ideas that gender is a binary and understand gender is a spectrum and that non-binary gender identities are real. These exclusionary attitudes aren't just perpetuated by cis people but by binary trans people too. They come from ideas that there are only two genders or that some genders aren't valid because of the way some people express their gender or choose to medically or socially transition. These are all personal choices and people are allowed to self-identify how they want without having to prove their identity. Ask not how your space can be inclusive for trans people but specifically for non-binary people too. Gender-exclusive spaces such as women's groups or men's groups can be necessary and made to be trans-inclusive for trans women and trans men; however, where are spaces for non-binary people to find peer support and share experiences in a confidential space with those who understand? There are many options that need to be discussed with the group. One option is to ensure the gender policy is made or adapted or have language updated to be more flexible to reflect the fluidity of gender identities: for example, a women's group for trans women and trans-feminine people. Another option would be to have a space for non-binary people only. Lastly, I'd consider asking again if a group needs to be separate by gender identities. Perhaps the group needs have changed if it started catering for binary genders, or, if there are anti-non-binary beliefs, there needs to be a conversation to address that.

Understanding sex diversity

Sex diversity is not spoken about as much as it should be, nor is it understood as much. I think this is because we are very familiar with the two sexes of 'male' and 'female', but we rarely speak about sex as a binary. The heavy focus and incorrect assumption that there are just two binary sexes means the people who fall outside of the sex binary are overlooked. Sex, like gender, is a spectrum. There are many sexes between the sex binary of male and female. The sex binary is another reductive binary that we need to challenge.

Following the definition of 'intersex' in Section 1, I will give an overview of what intersex solidary looks like and how to consider intersex people and people with intersex bodies or non-normative sex characteristics. Intersex people and young people must be believed. As children, many are left out of decisions about what happens to their bodies, do not have their own intersex bodies explained to them and are shamed for having non-normative sex characteristics. Ensure that intersex bodies are visible and celebrated as all bodies should be. Ensure that intersex bodies are a part of education on sex and biology.

In your spaces, challenge oppressive language and terminology with negative connotations (e.g. disease, disorder) and understand and educate others on what 'intersex' means. The more people understand what it means, the easier it will be to have conversations and to ensure that intersex is not a stigma, invisible or ignored. Whilst it is not explicitly included as a protected characteristic in the *Equality Act 2010*, some intersex conditions do fall within the protected characteristic of disability, so educating ourselves is a priority for knowing how best to support someone.

Anick Soni (2020), an intersex campaigner, shares how he wants us to support the intersex community: 'Never speak on behalf of intersex people or caregivers, there are many of us who are sharing our experiences globally. Most importantly, do not bring us up as an argument in debates about sex and gender – that's harmful to us. The best way to be an ally to the intersex community is to highlight, raise and empower inter-sex people to share their experiences. If you'd like to support the community, do some research on what the key issues are and find out what your local area does for intersex people.' Intersex-led organizations like Intersex Equality Rights UK and IIO have free information, toolkits and resources that can easily be shared and applied.

Where intersex and trans solidarity crosses over is in the same fight for bodily autonomy. It's up to all of us to protect, empower and support intersex communities.

Understanding class

Class is something I often find missing in conversations where it really matters. There's a resistance to name it amongst middle-/upper-class people (I include myself in this). There is a reluctance to see class privilege amongst us and in that we assume everyone has the same access and experiences and needs. I think class is difficult to explore because it is more than wealth or a socio-economic status – it's a dynamic. Class can change and does change, it carries geographic and regional nuance, it is racialized and gendered and it impacts our relationships with language, education and employment. What working class, middle class and upper class looks like is different because it infiltrates everything we do and influences all our experiences. Classism is experienced differently by people of colour than white people. Racism is experienced differently by working-class people than middle-class people. The intersections of class cannot be ignored.

The report 'We are ghosts: race, class and institutional prejudice' by The Runnymede Trust and The Centre for Labour and Social Studies (Snoussi and Mompelat, 2019) listened to London working-class communities on their experiences of racism and class prejudice, pushing back against the weaponization of the term 'working class' to create divisions between working-class people of colour and working-class white people. It gives four recommendations to make improvements for race and class inequality:

1. **Change the narratives:** stop equating race and class, acknowledge the legacy of colonialism in shaping modern-day Britain and contributing to the economy, don't put working-class communities against each other. We need to be careful – these echoes of such divides like white/poc, deserving/undeserving, British/migrants only justify policies that make all groups worse off.

2. **Rebuild the safety net:** an empowering narrative won't change the conditions of working-class people in the

UK. Improve security, pay and conditions of staff; give people seeking asylum the right to work; support workers – empower people by investing in their skills and treating them with dignity.

3. **Strengthen voice and participation:** involve working-class people in decision-making and developing services, invest in your local community organizations and networks who will already be engaging working-class and POC communities.

4. **Re-embed shared values at the core of policy:** embed inclusion, equality and cohesion across your organization. Whatever the system or services you have, working-class, migrant and POC communities need to be treated with care and dignity.

The findings from this report have also been developed into race and class messaging toolkits (The Runnymede Trust and The Centre for Labour and Social Studies, 2019) to build solidarity across difference and to discuss how to challenge 'divide and rule' narratives with 'what to say' and 'how to say' checklists, which I strongly recommend.

Angelo Boccanto for Media Diversity has covered this more recently in a feature 'Covid-19: race, class and the "great equalizer" myth' (2020). The coronavirus pandemic started conversations about the injustices faced by many communities. People spoke about the fact that front-line healthcare workers, care workers and transport staff are more likely to be exposed to the virus than the middle-class workers who have the privilege of working from home, but the fact that a disproportionate number of these workers are people of colour was often missed out. Charity So White, an organization dedicated to tackling institutional racism in the sector, produced a live position paper, 'Racial injustice in the COVID-19 response' (2020), highlighting the disproportionate impact of the pandemic, structural racism and socio-economic inequalities on POC communities in the UK. 'Without a purposeful, intersectional approach, centring BAME communities, the current outbreak of COVID-19 will lead to severe consequences and will further entrench racial inequalities in our society.' I would argue that this is advice that must be taken regardless of whether we are in a pandemic or an epidemic – the consequences will be felt and we must act now to shift class inequality in every way we can.

Agreements, contracts and policies

For trans POC, putting trust in services does not come easy; historically we are used to not being believed and our safety is not always made a priority when it comes to asking for help, especially when the support lies in hands of majority white or cis organizations. We see this through the nuances of safety and safe spaces, as explored in Section 2. For trans POC, confidentiality, listening, flexibility and belonging are the starting points. What does it look like when we implement this into agreements, contracts and policies?

Social justice facilitator, healer and doula adrienne maree brown has four universal tools when it comes to facilitating groups from organizations to collectives and alliances to networks (adapted from brown, 2017):

1. **Trust the people**

   This can be done by setting goals or intentions and being transparent about what these are, inviting the right people and facilitators to move the work forward, giving everyone room to say what they want to prioritize and talk about, developing an adaptable or living agenda so participants can shape the meeting, listening to everyone with love, giving the group time to be itself without your intervention and taking 'an elegant step': one that acknowledges the capacity of the group and what is possible and strategic.

2. **Principles**

   Shared and clear principles build a common understanding of what matters. What are the principles that are core to what you do? How can these principles be adapted to your group or community work? Are the principles adaptable and accessible? How do they open themselves up to change?

3. **Protocols**

   Protocols are ways that principles look in action. How is the work done? How do you show that you believe in the work? How do protocols show you working together and taking action together? Group agreements or working agreements are a great way to put principles into action.

   Brown shares her favourites for emergent spaces below:

   - 'Listen from the inside out, or listen from the bottom up (a feeling in your gut matters!);

   - Engage Tension, Don't Indulge Drama;

- W.A.I.T. – Why Am I Talking?

- Make Space, Take Space – a post-ableist adaption of step up, step back to help balance the verbose and the reticent;

- Confidentiality – take the lessons, leave the details;

- Be open to learning;

- Be open to someone else speaking your truth;

- Building, not selling – when you speak, converse, don't pitch;

- Yes/and, both/and;

- Value the process as much as if, I not more than, you value the outcomes;

- Assume best intent, attend to impact;

- Self care and community care – pay attention to your bladder, pay attention to your neighbours'.

4. Consensus
   'Make sure the people who will be doing the work agree on what is being done, why and how' (brown, 2017). Through practices like proposal-based decision-making, being honest about your level of agreement or giving a clear no, coming to a consensus can be efficient.

Our agreements and principles have to extend to all contracts and policies within an organization. Trans poc must be protected at all levels and not just within a tpoc group space

– what does protection look like for trans POC as members of, accessing other services within or being employed by your organization? How are trans POC kept safe? Ensure that their safety is thought of at all levels and not just the place they show up in. Some policies that are organization-wide many need to be examined from a trans POC lens, for example, safeguarding policies and the involvement of police, as explained in Section 1, also the involvement and application of the Prevent duty (*Counter-Terrorism and Security Act, 2015*), preventing people from becoming radicalized and predominantly safeguarding children, young people and prisoners.

The application of Prevent has in fact furthered discrimination against Muslim communities and LGBTQ communities through programmes such as 'No Outsiders' to promote LGBTQ education in schools. Prevent has been criticized by many groups representing British Muslim voices in the UK and more recently has been boycotted against the appointment of the chair (Grierson, 2021). Unison have published guidance called 'Responding to the Prevent Duty' (2016), which lists the concerns at the vagueness of the duty and the quality of training available, alongside widespread potential for Islamophobic and discriminatory behaviour and a breakdown in trust between staff and public service users. How are staff and workers implicated under this duty to report behaviour – can this be complemented with a supportive safeguarding board or safeguarding policy? How does this jeopardize your organization's practice, politics and ethics to implement something without problematizing it? How can problematic duties be positioned within the organization's own beliefs and policies? Ethical frameworks or guidance could be introduced as a way to hold policies and ensure they are in line with an organization's values.

When it comes to joining an organization as a participant, service user or client, what are they being asked to agree to? What are the prerequisites to accessing support? Do people need to show identification or 'prove' their identity? Consider the message this sends for people from TPOC communities where identity needs to be proven before they are given access to a service and how this is a replication of the anti-immigrant, racist and transphobic systems of oppression they navigate daily. Where you can make a choice to change and challenge a system to include more people, do it.

It is often just a name, title or gender marker on a membership form that is a huge barrier. For many trans people, their names, gender expression and proof of identity don't always match; it's not accessible for some trans people to have the funds or ability to make changes to reflect who they are. The bottom line is that trans people are who they say they are, and they need to be believed, especially when we are turning to an organization for support. Trans people also need assurance that the information they give will be respected by everyone. Take care to include the correct titles, gender markers or pronouns; misgendering someone contradicts asking for this information.

Lastly, personal details must be kept safe – confidentiality again must be guaranteed and may be nuanced depending on the size of the team or breadth of the services. What information is relevant, to who and why? The information a medical professional needs will be different compared to a creative workshop facilitator, and the information a yoga practitioner needs will be different to a youth worker. It should be clear and transparent why certain information around identity is being collected and if it is optional and if it needs to match a person's personal identification document. For example, someone's title (e.g. Mr, Ms, Mx) is not always necessary information to keep.

Acknowledgement and accountability

We can't get everything right. The aim of inclusion is not to get it right either, but to try. If we focus on getting it right, we lose focus of the communities we're doing it for. It's called inclusive practice for a reason – we are practising, doing inclusion regularly and repeatedly to improve at it. We can put everything into place and prepare for every eventuality, but we may still make a mistake – that is what we can and should prepare for. In fact, one of the most common pieces of advice that comes from learning allyship or solidarity is the importance of learning to apologize. To pre-empt the mistakes we can, we will and we do make, we must learn to apologize and take responsibility for our actions. This is a more constructive lesson than learning to get it all right. Considering how often things like terminology change, it would take a lot of time and energy to try and learn it all and keep up to date. Considering how fluid some parts of our identities are, it's also unlikely that the one fixed answer we have will fit all occasions. Learning to apologize can be integrated into an inclusive practice by building accountability into safe space agreements and policies.

Whether it is a mistake, problem or conflict, it requires nuance and will be contextual to the situation, the people involved and what can be done. Where possible, always seek to do things with others, as a team, collectively or with an external mediator. When it becomes something more harmful such as abuse or violence, always seek appropriate and timely action to ensure that safety of those at risk of harm or facing harm is a priority. (Incite! (n.d.) have a list of resources under Community Accountability to develop community-based responses and address violence in our communities, including activist- and poc-specific resources. See the References.)

When something goes wrong in a safe space, the group will be brought into question as responsible for the kind of space is has set up, including the facilitators or group members. What is the group dynamic that is set up – is the structure a hierarchy or flat or something in between? What does this structure do to those who want to challenge someone else either at the top or on the side? Is it explicit, clear or easy for the organization to be challenged or brought into question? What happens when the person involved is the person with the power – are there alternative routes, either internal, external or objective?

How accessible is the accountability process – is it clear that complaints, criticisms and suggestions are welcome? Is there an expectation that people with grievances will speak up? Is there an assumption that those people will be heard? How do privilege and power dynamics play into this? Have you built a structure/hierarchy that is able to be challenged, or have you just replicated a structure/hierarchy that keeps people with power in power?

Consider the dynamics of race, gender, class and more with these questions – again, the purpose isn't to find a correct answer. The questions will change as the context and community changes. Consider where trans poc can be included if they aren't already – consult with trans POC if this is an accessible and appropriate way to be accountable to their community. Think beyond safety; is this what trans POC need to feel like they can hold an organization accountable for when their safety is compromised or broken?

What happens when someone is hurt or a mistake is made? The immediate response is important and necessary despite what steps are taken next, hence why we do have to learn how to apologize. It is a reflection not only on us, our values or our organization and what it stands for, but a reflection also on how we view that person or community in front of us too. It's natural for our beliefs to be questioned by the person hurt or by ourselves when we see the impact of our actions.

When we think we are saying or showing we are sorry, what comes across could be very different. There are some common reactions, which I'll explore briefly, especially when it comes to '-isms', having your privilege exposed or being offensive or oppressive. These common reactions are defensiveness, guilt and shame. Section 1 covered some of this, exploring shame and privilege in detail. Here the focus is how to overcome oppressor guilt and move through it in the moment:

1. Apologize. Take a second, breathe, take another second and say, 'I'm sorry.'

2. Feel your feelings. Feel everything that comes from being challenged, questioned or called out on something you didn't do or something you didn't do well. I don't mean anger or defensiveness or fragility – I mean the feelings underneath that: shame, guilt, pain, disappointment,

powerlessness... These feelings will teach you about yourself, your position and what you will need next.

3. Think about apologizing again. Was your apology enough? Did you name the problem? Have you understood the other person's experience? Have you acknowledged your responsibility or role in this situation? If you feel you aren't responsible, was there something else that makes you complicit? Your silence or inaction? Or simply benefiting from white/cis privileges? White supremacy and cissexism may not be your fault, but you can still apologize for them when you play into them and hurt others.

4. Make space. Give yourself time to process away from the people involved with someone you trust who shares the same privileges or experiences. Give others space away from you to do their own healing, repairing and mobilization. Accept that you aren't in a position to make decisions or dictate what happens next; accept that the next steps may be without you. Ask 'What do you need?' if you haven't already been told and if you don't already know. Offer 'This is what I can do.'

5. Acknowledge it. Acknowledge racism/transphobia as the root of what happened. Label your behaviour for what it is, racist or transphobic, and see yourself as a piece of the puzzle in the bigger picture of white supremacy/gender oppression. It will be difficult and feel pretty awful to say this out loud, but the nature of oppression is that it is isn't meant to feel good to do the right thing, so we avoid doing it. We feed into it and remain in our position as

oppressors, and instead the oppressed experience is awful. Oppression thrives in ignorance and in shadows. It will fade quicker when we face it head on instead of hiding it under a cloak of denial.

6. Compassion and care. Take your time with this, but make sure you take this step. Compassion will help you overcome shame and care will help to build solidarity.

Maintaining a safe space

The key to maintaining a safe space is adaptability and longevity. Maintaining a safe space by adapting to community needs and feedback is part of the responsibility of providing safe spaces. With a flexible approach and avenues for feedback, this can be implemented easily.

When creating or using TPOC safe spaces, we must think about evaluating them too. How will you know it's working for TPOC communities right now and will work for TPOC communities tomorrow or next month? How will you know the space is still safe? Does safety still look the same? Gather feedback in accessible and creative ways with all trans people of colour at all levels of your organization, from service users, volunteers, frontline workers to board members, senior-level staff, trustees. Some groups review the agreement at the beginning of every group meeting, labelling it a 'working agreement' to show that it is a constant work in progress. Introduce it at the start of a group or meeting regardless of who is in the group and how familiar they are with the agreement. Make sure to ask for suggestions and reflections before moving on. Is there anything in particular to expand on for the particular event? Is there anything to focus on considering any current affairs or global events impacting TPOC communities? Demonstrate adaptability – a safe space doesn't always look the same, nor does safety always mean the same thing. Include new members and their voices – what do they need to make this space feel safer for them?

Think about adaptability across the board. Where else in your organization can you build processes for evaluating safe space policies or working agreements? Be critical and openly interrogate the approaches you are taking. What are TPOC experiences of sharing and giving feedback? The evaluation process requires trust; don't overlook that. How will TPOC experiences be heard? What does it feel like to measure safety? Are there ways of measuring that are reflective of the nature of the work? How do you quantify safety for TPOC communities? How is confidentiality, listening, flexibility and belonging captured and archived? Push back on words like success, achievement or performance, as these terms may alienate some with the connotations to productivity, capitalism and class oppression. What does 'success' really mean for TPOC safer spaces? Can there be space to celebrate instead the commitment to safe spaces?

Maintaining a TPOC safe space – making sure it is surviving and thriving – is caring for TPOC communities. Community care can be a part of longevity and ensuring the structures in place are lasting and sustainable.

'Shouting "self-care" at people who actually need "community care" is how we fail people', writes Nakita Valerio (2019) a writer and organizer, reminding us that self-care is not enough to care for our communities and to ensure our movements last. Community care is focused on the many, the collective, taking care of basic physical, emotional, spiritual and psychological needs through interpersonal acts to entire movements and protest. It's about prioritizing care, reducing harm and avoiding burnout through being together. Valerio (2019) writes, 'Ultimately, community care is a commitment to contributing in a way that leverages one's relative privilege while balancing one's needs. It's trusting that your community will have you when you need support, and knowing you can be trusted to provide the same.'

Section 4

Practice

How we take what we're learning and put it into action is all part of the practice. It is about building spaces and imagining worlds where trans people of colour are centred and celebrated. This is where liberation can start, as model and activist Munroe Bergdorf (2020) said, **'We show people what it is to be free.'**

Looking intersectional vs being intersectional

The visuals, images and photos on your website, offline material and publications will tell viewers who the organization represents and who it is for, as will the names and campaigns that are spoken about and shared. Whilst placing a trans Pride flag on a homepage or honouring International Transgender Day of Visibility with a hashtag is an easy and free action to show solidarity to trans communities, what are the intentions behind it? What are the motives when we put visible POC at the forefront of our campaigns and 'about us' webpages? Are we centring trans and POC communities in the same way when we aren't in front of an audience or on a public platform?

When doing public-facing work, it's always useful to question, no matter the size of the audience or action, whether you are taking an intersectional approach or if you are just focused on looking like you have done. When we think we are being watched or when we know there are people looking to us for guidance and role modelling, we can quickly turn that into thinking we are being judged and need to get everything right; the fear of getting it wrong can creep back in quickly and quietly. Our actions to support our communities must come from a genuine place of empathy and not from a place of fear or insincerity. This can lead us to token trans people, people of colour and other marginalized people to be the face/voice of a whole campaign or entire community, when they were largely unseen/unheard/unrepresented in the first place. 'Tokenism is the practice of cherry-picking a handful of societally underrepresented individuals, as a perfunctory effort to appear diverse and representative of the larger society', writes Ella Wilks-Harper (2016) on the fine line between tokenism and diversity. It's another way to exploit TPOC communities, neglect them and fail them.

Tokenism happens when organizations realize the lack of TPOC people within their service and how their service isn't catering to, representing or retaining TPOC, and their voices are missing. This is an uncomfortable truth that must be faced and responded to appropriately; be honest, centre TPOC and start an acknowledgement and accountability process.

Tokenism is most common when it comes to visuals. Whether it is campaigning or website branding, there are some things to consider when using images to empower and represent a community.

It's always more meaningful and accurate to have photos of the people you are actually supporting. There are of course issues around safety and visibility, especially for those at risk or accessing services where their identity needs to be protected. Consent to be in a photo should always be transparent and clarified, e.g. this first photo is for internal use only as a keepsake and this second photo will be for our Twitter page to promote this group. Offer different ways to be in the photo without being visible or identifiable, e.g. photos of just feet or hands or taken from the back. Participation can be empowering when TPOC are supported. Considering these issues around visibility of trans people of colour, common alternatives are illustrations and stock images to represent TPOC communities and services overall. Work with TPOC artists to illustrate people that represent the organization, ensuring visibility of diversity that's accurate. Work alongside equality and diversity working groups or LGBTQ/POC staff networks to ensure the process is being held by many to represent many. Consider starting a new working group that involves service users, members and volunteers to also have their say on what the visuals of an organization will look like and offer feedback. TPOC are familiar with the common stock photos that represent our communities – when accessing services to support us, we're faced with photos that further stereotype our experiences: a photo of an unhappy gender non-conforming person with stereotypically feminine clothing; a photograph of a pair of brown hands in handcuffs; a photo of a person of colour in a dark corner, alone and bruised – these images are disempowering. Images like these can add to stigma around getting help and perpetuate the shame and isolation we are already feeling. Photographs of chains, physical harm and sharp objects don't invite conversation; they narrow experiences and make it harder to seek support, saying this is what it looks like to be struggling. In addition to this, it sends a disempowering message to everyone that the only visible TPOC are alone, unhappy and oppressed. Where are the photos of empowerment, celebration and support? Diverse stock image banks exist. For example, The Unmistakeables (n.d.) released a free stock photography collection called 'Despora' representing the Desi diaspora in the UK as a way to address the underrepresentation of South Asians in the media and representing the community as it actually is.

Visibility

If you're looking for the best way to increase awareness of a campaign or service, one of the first things that will come to mind is visibility. Visibility is so important and it's more than just what we see. Visibility is about representation – it shows us the possibility that we can exist.

Dr Ronx Ikharia, a non-binary doctor and TV presenter, has a motto that captures this perfectly: 'You cannot be what do you not see' (Mitchell, 2021). If we cannot see something, we won't know it's there. It might sound obvious when talking about objects, but it applies to what we see in people too. There is a power in seeing ourselves represented too, whether that is a hidden identity or an unspoken experience.

> I found this survey via AORISTS [Anshika Khullar], the artist for the book *The Black Flamingo* by Dean Atta. Just being able to follow them on Twitter is nice, because it's nice to know there's someone else out there like me. Makes the world seem a little less lonely.

– survey respondent

Visibility is like a magnet. When we see a part of ourselves in someone else made visible, we are drawn towards it. When we see a possibility, it pulls us towards that too. It gives us permission to show our whole selves when we can see it in others. Whether it's face to face, in the media or online. Seeing trans people of colour across these platforms is seeing a possibility that we can exist anywhere and testimony that we **do** exist everywhere. Representation matters.

> It is really comforting to come across other BAME/POC enbies on Twitter.

– survey respondent

International celebrations such as International Transgender Day of Visibility (TDOV, 31st March) do more than centre transgender people: they highlight stigma we face daily, which tells others how to challenge transphobia and brings trans communities together all over the world exactly as they are. There's more on awareness days in Section 5.

Conversations about visibility often prompt a conversation asking the opposite: who isn't visible? Who are the people who are excluded and overlooked? This isn't the whole conversation. We must question who *gets* to be visible. Who are the people who are chosen to be, become, allowed to be included? When we look at visibility with an intersectional lens, we can also see it is not neutral; visibility, like safety, is a privilege.

Hierarchies still exist when we take care to include others. On TDOV the majority of trans people who front the campaigns and hashtags are white trans men and trans-masculine people. This visibility often serves those who are already most visible across communities: white people, men and masculine-presenting people. Only certain voices are visible; inclusive visibility is still needed. This happens because of privilege. However, visibility is not **always** a privilege.

Some trans communities have always been visible. Trans women and trans-feminine people, specifically from Black and Latinx communities, are hypervisible in our society. We know this because of how much they are (mis)represented in the media. Society sees them, but not for who they are. The documentary *Disclosure* (Feder, 2020) shows us that trans women have been misrepresented for decades in film and television, often playing into tropes as predators, criminals and sex workers. They have been written into scripts as targets to ridicule and mock; a twist of 'true' identity reveals but nothing than to further a plot. It might be more accurate to say that trans misrepresentation has been more visible for trans women of colour than they have been as a community.

In reality, trans women of colour are still targets. Misrepresentation has led to violence and harm upon these trans communities. Trans people are still fighting to be seen; however, visibility is not always a choice. The juxtaposition of Transgender Day of Remembrance (TDOR, 20th November), an international day of mourning for the trans community who have lost their lives through murder or suicide, shows us that hypervisibility also costs many their lives. The background of this day is also covered later in Section 5. Because of transmisogyny, trans women and trans-feminine people of colour are policed on what it means to be a woman and to be feminine and how they express themselves. 'I struggle to ignore the reality that the hypervisibility and hypersexualisation of black trans women in particular, has murderous consequences… The trans tipping point that Laverne Cox heralded from the cover of TIME magazine in 2014 has done so much to raise awareness and allyship. However, an anti-trans backlash has also been epic in its reach and impact. Year after year, it's the darker skinned women and girls who find ourselves being the most murdered', writes Kuchenga (2020) witnessing the effects of racism, anti-Blackness and transmisogyny on trans women and trans-feminine people of colour. A community that is profiled, their behaviours and appearance under further judgement. Visibility is not always a choice. And to be visible is not always safe.

This link between safety and visibility is crucial to understand. When we ask for visibility, we must demand safety. Some trans POC communities are indeed seen but are not safe. When we ask about visibility, we must ask, 'Who gets to be visible?' The trans people who are safe from misrepresentations, tropes and harm, are often the ones who hold privilege, who are white, cis-passing, able-bodied or in a higher socio-economic class or hold citizenship. Privilege gives you safety, and safety gives you privilege. This is why an intersectional lens is important to consider when it comes to visibility.

Online

As our lives continue to adapt to remote living and we rely more on virtual connections and communication, a website, online campaign or social media page may be the first step for someone to access support. Whatever platform on the internet you exist on, that platform is the first experience someone will have of who you are, who you represent **and** whether you represent them.

Think about how to make your online material inclusive and accessible by thinking about everyone who makes up trans POC communities, including disabled people, those with learning disabilities, those who are neurotypical, visually/audio impaired, young people and people at risk, migrants and people whose first language may not be English.

Confidentiality will be important to many trans POC, and for many this will include wanting to feel like this is a safe place for them and that they can trust they will be safe, as explored in the previous section. How can your website be a safe place? How can you build trust virtually? How does your website, landing page or social media profile build trust and a sense of safety? This can look like appropriate and fair (not tokenistic) representation of the communities you serve and accurate representation of the work that you do. This can look like publishing the confidentiality policies or safe space agreements of groups, assuring online visitors of what safety means for the organization and what the staff and members stand for. It can look like understanding who your online visitors may be and what they may be looking for. Safety starts online. Depending on your services, you may want to consider an 'exit button' that takes the visitor straight to another 'safer' website, such as a weather page or news site with one click.

Find out how your website or social page is doing: go behind the scenes to check analytics and visitor traffic to tell you what pages are the most popular, what countries people are visiting from, information about visitor ages and more. Consider translating the main pages and most visited pages to the languages either most spoken in your catchment area or that benefit the population you are serving. You can find information about this on the Office for National Statistics (ONS, n.d.) website, which has up-to-date census data and more. This will make it easier for people from different nationalities and backgrounds to find out necessary information; however, this might infer language support or translation services are available at the organization, so do consider if that is an accurate inference and needs to be clarified online or if another action should be taken to get translation support for your services. Translation services are becoming better online – some are built into web browsers, social media apps and offered by Google Translate – but don't rely on them. Consider human translation services too to get high-quality, accurate translations, especially for contextual and language nuances that is to be expected around gender/race discourse. When offline, ensure that it is clear whether groups or specific services are delivered in written or spoken English or if any facilitators or staff members are bilingual. Ensure all staff have knowledge and access to interpretation and translation services such as LanguageLine (n.d.), which can provide secure language services across industries. It's not about having the whole skillset – it's impossible to have everything and be everything – but having the assurance to know where the skills exist and where else they can be found.

As mentioned in Section 2, accessibility needs to be applied online too. When it comes to layout, fonts, colours and more, consult disabled-led organizations such as Diversity and Ability to improve and embed digital accessibility. Make sure that different formats (e.g. PDF, Word, hard copies via post, audio readings, etc.) are available for download; add alternative text descriptions to image/graphic posts ('alt text' functions are now available on many social media platforms, e.g. Twitter and Instagram); and add subtitles or transcripts for video content. Language is something that has been covered already in a few different ways, but, from an accessibility lens again, it's really important to consider language across online platforms and publications. Language represents your organization and who your services are for. Language and terminology can include/exclude people reading or listening to it, and the choices to use certain terms can be read as political and feel powerful. Sometimes an explanation as to why certain terms are used is helpful to understand what an organization stands for and their position to TPOC communities can be better understood. It's also an opportunity to be transparent and allow the community to shape the information that is describing them.

Writing in 'plain language' is an important part of accessibility and can be helpful to so many people. Examples of plain language include using short words with fewer syllables, commonly used words (avoiding jargon, formal or specialist language), using shorter sentences and shorter paragraphs for one or two ideas and using clear titles or headings. Lastly, try it and ask people for feedback, including those with different access needs and literacy levels. Take this further and consider doing an internal audit on your website, social media platforms and online materials checking for accessibility, inclusion and representation. Ask who your organization represents online versus who your organization supports and represents offline. How welcoming, trustworthy and affirming is the organization for TPOC when approaching it online for the first time? How likely are TPOC to access support and get in touch based on the online experience?

Venue

Whether your event is hosted in a building or on an online platform, the question to continuously ask yourself throughout is, 'Who can access this venue?' It's likely the venue will be accessible to some, not all. When it comes to accessibility, there's no such thing as 'fully accessible'. 'Fully accessible' implies accessible for all, however some needs simply by their nature counter other needs. For example, fluorescent lighting may be better for visually impaired people but may be debilitating for people with light sensitivity. This is why it's important to find out about access needs ahead of time and to ask and listen to the needs of your community. This may mean that certain requirements are prioritized, seen as essential or seen as optional. Who decides this? Are able-bodied people holding the decision-making power? Is this a transparent process? Requirements are not neutral. Whose voice, presence and needs are considered inconsequential?

Accessibility is not just about physical accessibility – consider financial accessibility too. Consider whether someone can afford transport to get to a venue, to pay for refreshments or a meal to get through the day or access technology or the internet. What bursaries can be offered to support travel, food, childcare or data packages? Will they require proof of income or be given with the belief that the people who need it are accessing it?

The venue itself can be a barrier to access and feeling welcome. Educational institutes, university buildings and places of worship may offer low-cost accessible spaces. However, these buildings are not neutral spaces and represent sites of oppression and exclusion for some. It's not always possible to seek alternative venues, but what is always possible is starting a dialogue with these venues. Use the power you have within an organization or collective to amplify the voices of others and make demands for accessible TPOC community spaces, gender-neutral facilities, changing rooms, travelling safely to and from venues and providing discretion. This is an opportunity to ensure that these venues are safe and accessible for TPOC in the future too and provide an opportunity for education and change.

It's more than just practicalities to consider with venues and working online. If there is a reception area, security staff or online hosts, they will be the first people to greet TPOC attendees. Speak with the staff in advance and brief them – take care of your TPOC attendees and your TPOC staff. Make sure they use appropriate language, handle any identification documents (where necessary) sensitively and, without being explicit about the group members' identities to protect confidentiality, let them know about trans identities, what that may look like (from diverse gender expression to names that may not match records) and that the best thing to do is to not make assumptions. Depending on the nature of the event, perhaps if there's an overnight residential or long-term work, a briefing or training session on gender diversity or trans awareness would be crucial to include as part of the booking process. Ask that all venue staff attend and make sure there is a trusted contact who can disseminate information and take on the feedback should any issues arise. Encourage them to implement these practices, from introducing their own pronouns to creating gender-neutral facilities.

Ahead of an event, provide written details of the venue and of what's available, including toilet facilities, changing facilities, ways to access the building (list how many staircases/ steps there are to enter the building/room, if there is a ramp, elevator, stairlift, etc.), ways to participate in the meeting (hearing loops, translators, etc.) local transport links, prayer spaces, seating areas and any refreshments available (with dietary/allergen information) and provide photos where you can. This isn't about showing off how inclusive you are or only sharing the things you've done to make the event accessible – share the things that are missing or what needs have been overlooked. Be honest so that people can make an informed decision about attending and make adjustments for themselves to attend.

Before sharing information publicly, think about safety again. Where is this information going and who needs to know? Attending events or entering buildings may inadvertently 'out' someone or have them associated with LGBTQ community or advocacy services, which could put them at risk.

Many cities do have a 'gay village', which can be an area of anxiety or risk for some, so be considerate. If is the first time someone is venturing into a visible LGBTQ area or if someone is not ready or safe to be labelled LGBTQ by association, this will impact who can access the space. Weigh up all the advantages and risks, keeping your privileges and the needs of the TPOC community in mind. Share important access information, but keep the address (or joining links and passwords if it's an online event) hidden until the day before the event.

Advertising and recruitment

Consider the history, usage and appropriateness of language, which words are visible and which words are used by the communities you want to approach or that you are offering services to. The power of language and labels will help others decide whether this is a space or service that will represent and include them. As with accessibility, get the support of human translators and consult with people from those communities. Use guides on gender-neutral language and consult with trans organizations about what terminology is empowering and correct at the time – don't assume what a community needs. Critique your position as a member/researcher/leader outside of that community looking in.

Take this forward and examine the process for someone coming to an event or service for the first time – what is the process like for newcomers? How welcoming is it or how straightforward is it? Is there a drop-in service, do you require registration or to take details or do attendees have to have a conversation with a worker, and who will be their point of contact?

When it comes to membership, application or monitoring forms, these need to be as inclusive as the service provided. Are they available in alternative formats and can they be returned in alternative formats? Whilst monitoring forms provide useful demographic data about service users, job applicants, employees and volunteers, they can easily be forgotten and not updated regularly to reflect the appropriate language or accommodate for the population accessing and representing your organization. Review monitoring forms with people of different experiences and backgrounds – consider taking it to an equality and diversity working group or LGBTQ/POC network to workshop. What data is being collected anonymously? Is it still useful? Is it accurate? Consider open-box questions to avoid literally othering people with an 'other' box when their options aren't listed. Consider what your organization is prepared to do with new and old data, where it can be stored accurately and confidentially, who can deliver regular reporting and when it can be reviewed again.

When it comes to inclusive recruitment, be creative and proactive. TPOC can struggle with imposter syndrome from the failings and experiences of employers and schools that institutionally discriminate and disempower them. Educational experiences and skills won't match those of white, cisgender and privileged counterparts, but these should not be any less valued. Think about how your application pack can be written to reflect this awareness and how the application can encourage TPOC applicants to draw on all kinds of experiences (not just in paid work or formal education) to fit a job description. Make the application pack more accessible, and have the potential line manager record a video. It's a chance to deliver information in a different format and for new people to see who and what the organization is. Encourage applications to be in different formats too, such as voice recordings or videos. Share this across social media platforms as well as with specific groups. Use your networks and contacts to share the job, be proactive in making sure that this reaches trans POC and take the chance to start building relationships, and listen to how it is received too.

Speak with LGBTQ/POC networks and local/national groups to share opportunities. Make it explicit in the application that applicants from TPOC communities are particularly welcome. Don't make this an empty gesture – where the role is isolated or they are the only trans person or person of colour in the team. Ensure there is appropriate TPOC supervision and training, staff TPOC networks to join and links to external TPOC networks to support their role. Recruiting for TPOC is more than just getting someone in the door – prevent tokenism: do the deeper work to invest in new recruits and retain TPOC staff. For more on recruitment, look into The Change Collective Guides for recruitment agencies, hiring managers, small charities and jobseekers to support your workforce and fundraising profession to become more inclusive, by The Chartered Institute of Fundraising (2021).

For many TPOC, especially young people, leaving the house or attending events online can be difficult if they are in an unsupportive environment or if they're not open about their identity to their family, guardians or carers. Those at risk of harm/isolation may need support and community the most, and alternative ways of contact and support such as a phone calls, emails or texts can be encouraging for them to know that they are still a part of the community and have the right to support.

What are the alternatives available, and are these explicit? Are there other ways to participate that are safe online, such as using headphones and keeping the camera off, or practically providing safe transport to and from the venue?

Partnership and funding

Partnership work can go hand in hand with any kind of outreach and it should do, as it's crucial to inclusive practice, that is, working with everyone who supports the TPOC community and benefits from TPOC-run services. Work with therapists, teachers, prisons, schools, musicians, creatives, GPs, young people and more. Work with TPOC communities by working with the people who speak with them. Ultimately, the experts on TPOC communities are TPOC communities. Work with them to build relationships, trust and solidarity. Understand again where your power lies as an individual, as an organization and as an individual within your organization. Use your power (e.g. capacity, time, funding) to support TPOC groups who are lacking in these areas so the objectives of TPOC community work can continue and develop. Support under-funded and un-funded TPOC collectives and creatives and invest in the TPOC community, which will benefit all involved.

When it comes to new projects for TPOC communities, be aware of the blind spots. As well as your own position outside these communities, take time to investigate if what you are doing is indeed new; it's likely that TPOC groups have tried similar projects already or the work is happening on a level that you're not privy to. There will be existing research, networks or relationships that we can learn from. Recalculate where the best place for your energy is, especially as someone white or cis; whether that means it becomes a partnership project or you hand over control to TPOC groups, ensure your work for TPOC is TPOC led. If there are no TPOC involved in work to support TPOC communities, or where the TPOC leading the work are volunteering/offered no financial remuneration, stop and reflect on why the work is happening, who asked for the work to be delivered and why TPOC labour and knowledge are being exploited.

Financial disparity across TPOC communities has led many to fundraise for themselves and others to call on the philanthropy and fundraising sector to do more to support TPOC groups. A lot of the inequality that exists needs to be addressed by funders. This was particularly noticeable during the Covid-19 pandemic reported on by Charity So White (2020) (position paper referenced in Section 3), who called on funders to ringfence funding for POC-led organizations. Martha Awojobi (2020), non-profit consultant, writes, 'Fundraising is so much more than writing bids to white-led foundations. Because of the myths surrounding people of colour's capacity to donate many organisations do not know that there are alternatives and there are huge benefits to being entrepreneurial when it comes to income generation.'

QTIPOC-led organizations such as Black Trans Foundation ran successful crowdfunding campaigns and have been able to provide funding for their own services for Black trans communities, staying independent of white-led foundations and restricted funding. Exist Loudly, an organization for queer Black youth in London, was so successful with crowdfunding that they were able to offer grants to Colours Youth Network, Gendered Intelligence, TPOCalypse group, Rainbow Noir, Unmuted Brum and Kamp Kiki – all QTIPOC-led initiatives and supporting QTIPOC communities, enabling them to continue the work they are doing whilst remaining completely QTIPOC led. Organizations such as Action for Trans Health ringfenced some of their fundraising income to support TPOC by starting a POC funding pot, used to roll out healthcare and wellbeing bursaries to TPOC only.

The link between inclusive practice for people of colour and funding is parallel to the link between being anti-racist and being anti-capitalist; how racial discrimination has been executed in the forms of exploitation, appropriation and colonization points to a form of racial capitalism, as they have all driven the economic growth of the UK and USA. 'In order to truly be antiracist, you also have to truly be anti-capitalist', says Ibram X. Kendi, author of *How to Be an Antiracist* (2019). This is further explored by the philanthropic network Justice Funders (2020); they continue to write on how we can dismantle white supremacy and anti-Blackness in philanthropy in response to increases in racist police violence around the world, and invite you to reflect on the following:

- How do white supremacy and anti-Blackness show up in my individual and institutional mindsets and behaviours, and how have I/my institution been complicit in perpetuating these systems of oppression?

- What steps can I/my institution take in this moment to support those most impacted by white supremacy and anti-Blackness?

- How is my institution currently supporting (through grants and investments) the systems that are harming our communities, including the police and prison industrial complex?

- How does my personal stance and my institution's stance

on defunding the police and prison abolition impact the ways in which we are responding to this moment?

- How might we align and move more resources to Black-led organizing work and grassroots leadership to meet this moment AND commit long-term support to this work?

- How am I/my institution leveraging this moment of upheaval to create the new, just world we all need?

Justice Founders (2020)

Section 5

Celebrate and Commemorate

There is so much to celebrate and honour in the lives, both lost and present, of trans people of colour. Travis Alabanza (2017) writer and performer wrote:

Trans femmes are the past, present and future
We are all the possibilities ur world could be
We are deserving of your love, protection, affection

All our communities are richer because of the contributions of Black trans people; trans women and trans femmes of colour; trans people of colour, faith and religion; neurodivergent trans people of colour; and trans people of colour with disabilities. We can learn so much from TPOC his/her/their-stories, so let's make sure we do.

National celebrations/awareness days

The nuance of visibility, safety and privilege is something to carry through to national celebrations of LGBTQ and POC communities as well as awareness days of issues that affect us. For ease, I'll refer to them here as campaigns, and everyone will have a different relationship to them.

What is the intention when taking part in this campaign?

The first thing to consider is the intention. This will help shape what the campaign looks like and who it is for. What do you want? What is your organization hoping to achieve? And are these intentions from a place of good faith, obligation or fear? Be cautious of 'performative allyship' – taking part in campaigns just to look like an ally without doing the work of being an ally. A clear example of this is the #BlackOut-Tuesday campaign on Instagram, which very quickly became a performative allyship trend. Non-Black people who have been largely silent on racial discourse started posting a black square on their profiles and using hashtags that community members and Black activists use to find resources, resulting in a literal blackout of important and necessary information. Questioning these actions to find out the intentions behind why this became a trend, such as to listen or learn or show they care, means we can find other ways to support the Black community without further tokenizing, harming or silencing them.

Who is taking part in this campaign?

Take note of the people who are leading the campaign; who is the driving force behind it? Campaigns should be led by the people they affect and represent and driven by people with that lived experience. White trans people or cis people of colour alone will not be able to lead inclusive campaigns for trans people of colour without working with trans people of colour. In addition, this doesn't build trust or faith for TPOC viewing the campaign, because it raises the question of why TPOC aren't involved, and, following that, why is the campaign happening without them?

Partnership work is key, but who you partner with will also drive the response and audience. TPOC communities will have negative relationships with organizations and institutions, and the way to understand what these are and avoid further harm is to consult with those TPOC communities and invite them to be the driving force instead. This is often seen when companies or big organizations partner with others linked to anti-trans or racist actions – communities respond by boycotting events or products as the partnership (usually with some financial benefits for the discriminating group) sends a message that TPOC communities are not protected, their experiences are not believed and their voices are not important enough to partner instead with organizations who actively empower trans people and people of colour.

What does the community need?

If you have reflected on your intentions and have TPOC leading and heading a campaign, go back to consultation and make sure you have asked directly and explicitly: do TPOC want this campaign? Have TPOC asked for more awareness or commemoration on a certain issue, or is this something that white or cis organizations have assumed a community needs? One of the reasons why campaigns are so powerful is that they come from the community themselves. Non-Binary People's Day (14th July) was proposed by Katje van Loon, a non-binary Canadian feminist, in 2012 as a day that focuses on non-binary contributions to the world without being grouped with men or women; chosen as the exact middle date between International Women's Day (8th March) and International Men's Day (19th November), it is now internationally recognized to celebrate non-binary communities and raise awareness in the week leading up to it. Community needs may even be based on a historical consultation or from research in another part of the country or world, but what a TPOC community needs **here and now** may be different – needs change. We need to respond to that and be flexible in our approach. The answers might reveal that energy is better placed in direct action right now instead of planning an awareness week later in the year, as an example. The TPOC community will always know what the TPOC community needs.

What can we do for the community?

This is a question to be asked in parallel with asking what the community needs. Knowing our privilege is a prerequisite to this question; it's about knowing the true influence, power and capacity we have on an organizational and individual level. This is about being realistic and honest about what can be done to celebrate and commemorate TPOC communities.

This is a question to be explored within organizations too – it should not be more work for TPOC communities to tell us what they think we can do. It doesn't have to be something we do alone either.

Author Reni Eddo-Lodge talks about 'The Big Question' on her podcast titled *About Race* (2018c) when asked, 'What can we do?' What can we do as allies to fight racism, what can non-Black people of colour do, what can the trans community do for intersex solidarity, what can we do for non-binary people? Eddo-Lodge continues to say, 'I don't know where you hold influence in your life. I don't know your friends, I don't know the extent of your jobs, I don't know where you can assess where the institutional racism is really taking hold in your sector, what you as individuals can attempt to do to try and change that. I'm in no position to tell you how you can try and change the problem. But in terms of where you hold influence in your lives? In order to attempt to overcome the problem, only you can diagnose that.' So, what can you do?

What are we prepared to do next?

Intentions matter and speak volumes, but actions are louder. A campaign needs to be more than taking part. Don't let a momentum build just to be let go of and abandoned. The momentum is part of a movement; what exists beyond what's attractive, trending and popular? A community exists beyond one day, week or month of awareness-raising, and a community will need us beyond that too. What are we doing after we celebrate TPOC to ensure the movement is sustainable? How do we keep TPOC movements alive, and literally, how do we keep trans people of colour alive? Are we there in moments of mourning **and** are we celebrating life, honouring through rejoicing? Let community members hold us accountable for our actions and staying true to our word.

> Help the trans POC community – a minority within a minority. Our voices are not forgotten.
>
> – survey respondent

Mireille Cassandra Harper, writer, has a succinct guide on how we can be anti-racist with non-optical allyship (2020). Optical allyship, a term coined by author and doula Latham Thomas (2018), refers to allyship and actions that only serve at a surface level and aren't concerned with going deeper to the root of oppression. It platforms the 'ally' instead – it is performative allyship where the solidarity we offer is superficial. Non-optical allyship includes the importance of understanding what optical allyship is, checking in on TPOC friends, family and community during traumatic and difficult times, being prepared to do the work through your own privilege, shame and guilt. Also, educating yourself, read/watch/learn anti-racist and gender liberation material; donating to TPOC funds and initiatives; avoiding sharing content that is traumatic and triggering for TPOC; avoiding centring this narrative around yourself, your personal journey or how you relate; continuing support after the outrage; stopping support for organizations or platforms that promote hate; and starting a long-term strategy to make a long-term impact and meaningful change.

Annual calendars

The calendar that follows (Table 5.1) is an example only: it's unfinished and incomplete, and it's intended as a starting point. Whilst this is made with the UK in mind, some USA holidays have been included as they often provide opportunities to talk about the British Empire and the slave trade, for example, which don't get spoken about enough. Draw up calendars for your organization, ask for contributions from your team and community members, ask for the events and milestones they want to commemorate, add events that are specific to your country and faith. Create one that is representative of your communities. Be creative and intersectional; for example, celebrate International Youth Day by centring trans youth of colour and the organizations and TPOC youth workers who support them. Another example would be to celebrate World Refugee Day by raising awareness of the experiences of trans POC migrants and how we can show solidarity to them.

Some days will differ year to year within the UK and across the world, so double check in advance. Use this as an opportunity to reach out to local charities to find out if they're running any campaigns, and ask what you can do to help raise awareness or support your communities together. More recently, groups take advantage of awareness days and extend them into awareness weeks or even months. Remember to take into account religious celebrations and awareness days affecting other marginalized communities – these will also affect LGBTQ and POC communities.

Table 5.1 An example calendar of cultural, historical and social events

January	27th Holocaust Memorial Day
	Every 3rd Monday Martin Luther King Jr Day (USA)
February	4th Rosa Parks Day (USA)
	21st International Mother Language Day
March	8th International Women's Day
	10th Harriet Tubman Day (USA)
	16th Young Carers Action Day
	21st International Day for the Elimination of Racial Discrimination
	25th International Day of Remembrance of the Victims of Slavery and the Transatlantic Slave Trade
	31st International Transgender Day of Visibility
April	2nd World Autism Awareness Day
	6th International Asexuality Day
	22nd National Stephen Lawrence Day (UK)
	26th Lesbian Visibility Day
	Every 3rd Friday Malcolm X Day (USA)
May	1st International Workers Day
	17th International Day Against Homophobia, Transphobia and Biphobia (IDAHOBIT)
	19th Agender Pride Day
	24th Pansexual and Panromantic Awareness and Visibility Day

Cont.

June	19th Juneteenth (Emancipation Day) (USA)
	20th World Refugee Day
	Every 2nd week National Carers Week
July	14th International Non-Binary People's Day
August	12th International Youth Day
September	10th World Suicide Prevention Day
	23rd Bisexual Awareness Day
October	10th World Mental Health Day
	11th National Coming Out Day
	26th Intersex Awareness Day
	Every 3rd Wednesday International Pronouns Day
November	8th Intersex Day of Remembrance
	13th–19th Transgender Awareness Week
	20th Transgender Day of Remembrance
December	1st World AIDS Day
	2nd International Day for the Abolition of Slavery
	17th International Day to End Violence Against Sex Workers
	18th International Migrants Day

(List of minor secular observances, 2021; list of multinational festivals and holidays, 2021)

History months

History months are about many things such as education, celebration and commemoration. They're an opportunity for schools, universities, workplaces and charities to share histories that aren't often known, to spotlight local LGBTQ and Black trailblazers and role models, and to take the opportunity to do more for the LGBTQ and Black people they work with or support. From running panel discussions and campaigns and launching resources to running a new curriculum or extracurricular activities or partnering with LGBTQ and Black organizations, there are many ways to honour history months. In the UK, February marks LGBTQ **History Month** and October marks **Black History Month**. In 2019, the UK launched **South Asian Heritage Month** in July, an opportunity to explore how intertwined British history is with South Asian history, to exchange stories, build relationships and speak on the injustices happening within the community.

Ruby Bukari (2020), one of the event coordinators of the first South Asian Heritage Month, writes, 'There is a clear demand for further investigation and conversation on gatekeepers, colourism, systematic and structural racism and lack of opportunities.' Commemorating history and heritage should not shy away from the injustices of slavery, colonialism and imperialism that have shaped TPOC communities and identities today. Instead, confront the discomfort and do not allow history to repeat itself by learning from it. History months do face criticism from LGBTQ, Black and POC communities when this doesn't happen – where we are erased and silenced once more, misheard and misrepresented. History months can easily miss many of the same nuances and planning that have been previously mentioned when delivering campaigns.

Approach history months with an intersectional and critical lens. Look back on the history that we have been taught and view it with a trans or gender-diverse lens or a Black lens. Where are trans people of colour within history? Just because they aren't on the page in front of us doesn't mean they weren't there or contributing to the history we are told. Be critical and be curious; history is not neutral or objective. It shows when we only platform white celebrities and historical figures during LGBTQ History Month, or when we only have predominantly men, cisgender people or non-Black people of colour during Black History Month. We are not just celebrating one identity or one community during these months. When we don't celebrate the whole community, the whole community is not being seen. Trans people of colour and Black trans people have contributed so much as activists, fighters and speakers, and it's the same systems of oppression that they were fighting that erase their contributions from history.

There's so much connection in the fight for human rights, and historically, LGBTQ and Black movements have supported each other. Black LGBTQ activists shaped the civil rights movement: Bayard Rustin, Stormé DeLarverie, Ernestine Eckstein, Phill Wilson, Miss Major Griffin-Gracy. And trans women of colour led LGBTQ movements: Marsha 'Pay It No Mind' Johnson, Sylvia Rivera. The Stonewall Uprising (also known as the Stonewall Riots) has been documented and retold as an event that defined the LGBTQ rights movement that we know today. However, that was not possible without the dedication and leadership of trans women of colour committed to the survival and rights of LGBTQ homeless youth, sex workers and people of colour. Acknowledge the failings of archivists, curators and storytellers. When we can only find the same white, cisgender or heterosexual stories, we can speak out about the erasure or omission – this in itself tells a story. Do not continue cycles of erasure and include the activists and changemakers who are still missing, such as youth, disabled and intersex voices. We must preserve TPOC legacies and ensure we know that they have paved the way for all of us to be here today.

> When Black History Month is finished we don't stop being black. When LGBTQ history month is finished, we don't stop being LGBTQ. (Lady Phyll, founder of UK Black Pride, in Bartholomew, 2019)

REFLECT ON

- Who is your history month for?
- How can you make your history month more inclusive when history itself has been exclusive?
- Where are TPOC stories passed on and how can we support this?
- How can we contribute and preserve truer his/her/their-stories of TPOC?

Pride

Pride events for any community are a celebratory time of year. History also matters here, as Pride events have generally arisen from protest. Pride is a time to mark accomplishments and community wins and to mark that Pride still is a protest for many.

The importance of Pride events for so many members of TPOC communities highlights the importance of making an inclusive Pride event. These events are safe spaces of acceptance, belonging, joy, liberation and connection. Pride is not just for one community or experience. Pride is for the many. Hugely successful events like UK Black Pride for all LGBTQ POC have shown that you can centre more than one community, and the rising numbers of attendees in London each year show how many feel welcome and included.

Pride events also bring in criticism from TPOC communities – similar to challenges raised about history months and campaigns around their questionable long-term goals, intentions and representations. Pride is about the people, but it's also a community event and a collaboration – it's easy to forget that there is collective power as well as individual power. When organizations listen to these challenges and questions, they can have a great influence and prompt great change elsewhere too.

The LGBT charity Stonewall has been a major partner with Pride in London for London Pride events for years. In 2018 Stonewall released a statement that they will be partnering instead with UK Black Pride, a deliberate action to support LGBTQ POC communities and a response to the lack of POC diversity and inclusion at Pride in London, as well as a lack of public acknowledgement: 'We know that racism is a real issue across LGBT communities and Stonewall has committed to a major programme of work on black, Asian and minority ethnic (BAME) inclusion. The board has therefore decided to significantly extend our support and participation in UK Black

Pride this year... Our focus on this event is a reflection that racism is a serious problem across LGBT communities, and that we want to be part of the solution – learning from BAME activists and supporting organisations like UK Black Pride in their work' (Stonewall, 2018).

REFLECT ON

- Who are your sponsors or partners? Where do they stand on TPOC rights and representation? What are TPOC experiences of those sponsors or partners? What does it mean, then, to TPOC to accept money or grants from such companies?

- How can you redistribute wealth? How can you challenge buying into 'the pink pound' or the LGBTQ market and challenge exploitation of TPOC communities with free/affordable events and travel/accommodation bursaries?

- How accessible is your marketing material for TPOC communities? Is it discreet so can be shared easily? Is it available in different languages or different formats? Do the Pride flags, photos and language used represent TPOC?

- If there is a march or walk, how accessible is it for disabled communities? Are there other ways to participate and join protests? Who is at the front?

- How safe is it for TPOC communities? Is there a police presence? Can alternative methods of security and protection be sourced? What is being done to make Black people, people of colour, trans and gender-diverse people feel safe?

- How is your organization celebrating Pride season internally and externally? What can you do to make sure you don't fall into performative or optical allyship?
- How is your organization supporting TPOC communities after Pride season internally and externally?

Yes, Black Lives Matter

This is not a debate, nor an event or trend. Black Lives Matter is a social justice movement and a demand for the lives of all Black people to be valued, protected and loved. If we are committed to tackling racial discrimination and seeking social justice for our communities, this must be understood and any misinformation must be challenged. This is not saying anything new – justice has been demanded for as long as anti-Blackness and racism have existed. Organizations in the USA, the UK and across the world have increasingly used the Black Lives Matter movement to protest and counter violence at the hands of the state and centre Black safety and liberation.

When people say Black Lives Matter, it is often contested as an exclusionary or divisive phrase, as if they are saying **only** Black Lives Matter or that white lives don't matter. These debates derail from the core of the message and the uncomfortable realities of the racist society that we are a part of. We can change that by understanding what is really being said with this statement. Shaka Hislop (2020), retired footballer and honorary president of 'Show Racism the Red Card', explains more and why saying 'all lives matter' is offensive: 'Rooted in the days of slavery and colonialism, where, without question, black lives simply did not matter, through to today, where they don't seem to matter as much. Nobody involved in the Black Lives Matter movement is saying that **only** black lives matter, or that all lives don't matter or that white lives don't matter. The issue with that is that white lives have always seemed to matter **more**, and in some circumstances, they've been held supreme, hence the term white supremacy. What "Black Lives Matter" is saying is that all lives matter equally. Black lives have to matter just as much as everybody else's.'

Centring Black Lives Matter campaigns and movements in your organization means centring Black people in the organizations that you work with or support, Black organizations you work alongside, Black groups and businesses in your local area, education on Black history, anti-Blackness and your position of privilege and power within these systems of oppression. Don't tokenize or appropriate Black movements by playing into optical allyship. Understand how movements work and make sure that the change you're a part of is sustainable and meaningful. Posting black squares for #BlackOutTuesday across social media or platforming Black voices for a day/ week/month in response to a death of a Black person at the hands of the police is not enough, not just because it is performative. These peaks of action and demonstration are only part of the movement cycle. Nim Ralph (2020), community activist and trainer, explored this with the movement cycle (see Figure 5.1) in a series of tweets:

> When looking at movements throughout history they have a typical cycle of energy and activity. Most people think of a movement as existing in its 'uprising' and its 'peak'. These are

stages when there has been a 'trigger moment' that kicks off rapid change and attention.

There are lots of types of trigger moments but right now are unprecedented times in my lifetime and we are living through a few simultaneously (on different scales) e.g. COVID-19 and global lockdowns, the murder of George Floyd, the reform of the GRA and many more.

A movements life cycle doesn't stay in the peak – it moves into 'contraction' and 'evolution' – these stages of a lifecycle can be wholly demoralising because to the people directly affected it feels like no one cares anymore.

Emotional states rise significantly in uprising and peak but collapse quickly when the movement meets its contraction stage. But these moments also lead society into a state of creating a 'New Normal' and regrowth for the movement.

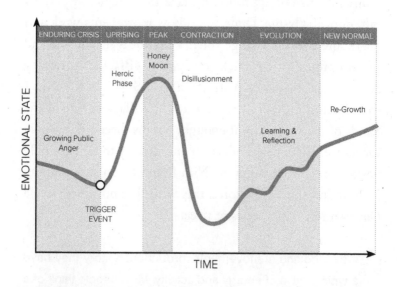

Figure 5.1 The Movement Cycle

The Movement Lab (2016)

What can we do to continue care during the learning and quieter reflective stages of the cycle? What can we do to ensure we stay on track for regrowth? How can we empower Black voices to shape a new normal? Movements are not always visible. A cycle is not always smooth. The movement needs to be kept alive and so do our TPOC communities.

Section 6

Exclusion and Inclusion

Drawing from my own personal experiences, quotes from survey respondents and some case studies, this section puts the theory into real-life practice.

One of the ways we learn is through mistakes, but these mistakes do not always need to be our own.

Starting with 'Exclusion', I explore some of the ways language, names and pronouns, and harmful stereotypes and performative allyship exclude trans people of colour with some alternative and preventative suggestions.

There are so many simple and creative ways we can include trans people of colour too. Think outside the (tick) box. Following this is 'Inclusion', a small showcase of the many ways others are making space for inclusive leadership in faith communities, committing to trans inclusion, having conversations about whiteness, taking responsibility for failings and doing youth work led by TPOC. These examples are not perfect or absolute. What an individual or organization can do will still be unique. However, there are some points that can be taken and applied to most; you will find a list of ten ways to make your practice inclusive to round off this section.

Exclusion

Hiding behind language

> I'm asked to be used in photoshoots at work a lot, often used as 'an Asian voice' for young Asians when really they want a South Asian person and not an East Asian person.
>
> – survey respondent

When a broader term like 'Asian' is used as a catch-all term to imply a broader representation, it falsely implies that it is truly representing all Asian voices, when in fact the only voices represented and desired are South Asian voices. Campaigns are more concerned with looking inclusive and like they are supporting many communities, hiding behind broader terms to avoid having to actually be inclusive and acknowledge they are only supporting a small number of people. This is similar to how the term 'people of colour' can be used when only one identity is being spoken about or represented, which is often an identity that is relatively over-represented, such as the South Asian identity, illustrated here.

This also applies to acronyms like BAME events – where no Black voices are included in the formation or leadership – and LGBTQ events – where no steps to include trans people have been taken. When a group of people have already been excluded, there's not much that can make that better in the immediate moment. However, the response and reaction will make a difference; being honest about the limitations of the event will enable people to know what to expect and then they can make an informed decision about whether to participate. Having a process where it's clear that responsibility is being taken by explaining why this has happened will build trust with communities by being transparent, and it will reveal to the organization where the gaps are and what needs to happen to ensure it doesn't happen again.

SUGGESTIONS

- Accurately describe who the campaign/event represents or is for and explain why.
- If voices are missing and this has been an oversight, acknowledge this and, again, explain why.

Names and pronouns

> Not being able to change my name at college on the system but other friends have changed their register name to their nicknames.
>
> – survey respondent

> There is no introduction of pronouns in the room.
>
> – survey respondent

It's dehumanizing for trans people to be denied their name and identity. In addition to this, having to introduce their pronouns and step into the educator role, alone, instead of being able to participate like everyone else in the room is exhausting and exposing. Trans people are already at risk, and to further draw attention to their trans identities by correcting their names, pronouns or explaining why that matters increases risk of discrimination. In a room where pronouns are not being introduced and where a trans person's name is actively being denied, it doesn't give confidence that that person is safe there. Cis people generally don't have to worry about their gender/ pronouns/nicknames being questioned, and their comfort and needs are prioritized. Trans people have a right to be called by their preferred name just as much as cis people have a right to be called by their preferred name, if not more, as trans people getting dead-named and misgendered repeatedly has a painful impact.

SUGGESTIONS

- Everyone is to introduce themselves with names and pronouns as a regular habit at the start of meetings and communication. Embed a practice that asks and doesn't make assumptions. It shifts the responsibility from trans people onto cis people too – everyone has pronouns, so everyone should be sharing them.

- Consult with trans organizations who work with schools to make registration more inclusive for alternative names and gender markers, and make sure this is done in a way that keeps the trans student safe – ask them privately and always double check before addressed letters are sent to the home address. The needs of trans young people must come first.

- Cis people, show your support and when you see unfairness;

name it and take action – amplify the needs of trans people where they are not being heard.

Non-binary exclusion

> After a post about Billy Dee Williams using 'male and female pronouns' on a Facebook page, when non-binary folx in the comments explained pronouns are not inherently 'male' or 'female' they got harassed. Either admin don't check the comments on their posts or they agree with the crowd and don't care about non-binary folx. Honestly, I'm just...so tired. I had to unfollow the page.
>
> – survey respondent

> This is a small thing but it seems to be getting worse: so many groups keep lumping non-binary folx in with women (i.e. 'women and non-binary') thinking it's being inclusive, when really it's just lowkey offensive. Someone on Twitter said it was because these groups think non-binary folx are just 'women lite' and honestly it feels like that. If people could stop doing that...that'd be real nice.
>
> – survey respondent

The impact of constant non-binary exclusion is real; it's tiring having their experiences, opinions and identities invalidated. Pronouns are not gendered; although they do indicate which gender someone may be, they are simply masculine, feminine or neutral. These uphold cissexist ideas that oppress trans and non-binary people.

When it comes to making women's spaces inclusive, they

often do the opposite and exclude trans men, trans women and non-binary people, perpetuating the reductive stereotype that trans people are their genitals, and that makes them more or less unsafe or dangerous. It doesn't make the space safe at all. Ultimately it means non-binary people here aren't being recognized, making the assumption that non-binary people are assigned female at birth, erasing non-binary people assigned male at birth. The way the 'women and non-binary only' rule is set up also excludes trans women and trans-feminine people. See Section 2 on exclusion policies based on gender.

SUGGESTIONS

- Actively care for non-binary people by asking how you can do this, listening to them and putting it into action.
- With gender exclusion policies, question why you are grouping people based on gender – if it is actually based on assumed genitals or gender history, and why that dictates how safe or unsafe as space is.

Playing into tropes of trans people

My old work got an offer from a filmmaker, a gay cis man, to make a film to use in their homophobia/biphobia/transphobia school campaigns. They asked me at very short notice if I had any advice on the storyline – a trans girl being bullied at school. I was the only out trans worker. They suggested I come on set, I couldn't so I shared guidelines (via All About Trans) of working with trans stories in media and which pitfalls to avoid like cis men playing trans women. The only trans people who had been consulted was their LGBTQ youth group. They said it would cost too much money to have a trans actor. The final clip showed a young trans girl played by a young cis man of colour putting on lipstick and having a hard time from her teachers. This wouldn't have happened if more trans voices were included from the start. As an educational video, it needs to represent trans youth fairly.

– survey respondent

It's good to have projects about LGBTQ youth led by LGBTQ youth, but with group consultations it's not clear how many trans youth were there in the above example, nor how many of their voices were included in the final decision, i.e. they may have been spoken over by cis young people and cis staff. It's the duty of an organization to represent people who aren't there, and it looks like it was an afterthought/tokenistic to include the trans employee in the trans storyline.

The nature of the film was to raise awareness of bullying, but it shouldn't have come at the expense of disempowering or misrepresenting communities. Cis actors playing trans roles – and especially cis men playing trans women – is such a harmful trope that links directly to the violence against trans women. Jen Richards, writer, explains the importance of casting trans actors to play trans characters in the documentary *Disclosure* (Feder, 2020): 'When you see these women off-screen still as women, it completely deflates this idea that they're somehow men in disguise.' These actors playing into 'the transness of it' turn gender into an exaggerated performance of femininity, such as described by putting on lipstick, as if wearing lipstick is their whole trans identity.

SUGGESTIONS

- Consult with trans people throughout a media project about them: young people, youth workers, community experts. Take time to understand the experiences of young trans women of colour navigating school, relationships with teachers, parents and self. It should not be a rushed process; consultation and feedback should be built into the timeline.
- Cast trans actors to play trans roles, trans women to play cis women and trans men to play cis men, and give opportunities for trans people to represent themselves authentically and be represented fairly. If funding/budget is an issue, consider the risks to the trans community when the film launches.
- Trans representation can be liberating for everyone if it breaks free of trans tropes and limiting gender stereotypes.

Performative allyship and BLM hypocrisy

Munroe Bergdorf, model and activist, was employed as the first trans person to be the new face of L'Oréal in 2017; however, L'Oréal ended their partnership with her after she called out racism and white supremacy following a violent white supremacist rally. She was accused by many of calling all white people racist, was told that her comments went against L'Oréal's values and was left with no support from them following death threats, rape threats and online harassment.

In 2020, Bergdorf came back at L'Oréal for hypocrisy after they posted a branded message in solidarity with the Black Lives Matter movement 'with no duty of care, without a second thought. I had to fend for myself being torn apart by the world's press because YOU didn't want to talk about racism.

You do NOT get to do this' (in Hou, 2020). Shortly after, Bergdorf received an apology, open dialogue with the brand, donations to UK Black Pride in support of LGBTQ POC and Mermaids in support of trans youth and has joined L'Oréal's diversity and inclusion board. Bergdorf said, 'I thought that it would be the perfect opportunity to practice what I preach and take up that seat at the table and to be the representation that we deserve as a community. I believe in accountability and progress, not cancellation and grudges.'

SUGGESTIONS

- Understand that racism and transmisogyny will mean that extra support and care is needed for trans women of colour and that organizations have a duty of care for these communities if they are to genuinely be concerned about diversity and justice.
- Listen to Black trans people about their experiences of racism, white supremacy and anti-Blackness, and believe them.
- Learn about white supremacy as a system that isn't about people as individuals – it's about a whole system, society and economy that operates from it and that white people benefit from. Educate other white people as white people.
- Keeping open to accountability and dialogue will make greater change and benefit greater communities.

Inclusion

Inclusive leadership in faith communities

Faith communities are often stereotyped as being oppressed

or oppressive, stereotypical and traditional with gender roles and expectations. This is no truer than any other community in society, and often these views are seen through a white or Islamophobic lens. The Inclusive Mosque Initiative (IMI) was founded in 2012 as a radical and inclusive mosque space for people from marginalized communities and to build solidarity too. They make their beliefs and stances clear to the public and practise this in their events, from having dedicated spaces to discuss gender and prayer in balanced, safe ways and having events for all genders, to using all pronouns for Allah and prioritizing women, trans and non-binary people and those from Muslim minority backgrounds to lead prayer. The IMI explains further in their statement of intent:

> The Inclusive Mosque Initiative is dedicated to creating places of worship and spiritual practice for marginalised communities, and to the promotion of inclusive Islamic principles. In this, we are committed to centring and uplifting the voices and experiences of marginalised people within our communities, and creating inclusive, safer spaces.
>
> To us, that means having a critical awareness of the dynamics of power and privilege, and working against racism (including anti-Blackness, Islamophobia, anti-Semitism), homophobia, gender-based discrimination, poverty, ableism, and environmental damage and all the ways these intersect.
>
> In particular we express solidarity with immigrant, refugee, disabled, working class and poor, Black and brown people, and we are critical of the State violence enacted on these communities through excessive surveillance, police brutality, the prison industrial complex, national borders, poverty and

the Prevent duty, to name a few. In connection to this, we do not accept government funding.

In this process we are committed to learning from each other and welcoming differences of opinions and practice, and are willing to be held accountable by our community to ensure we uphold these values. (Inclusive Mosque Initiative, 2016)

Commitment to trans inclusion

Martha Awojobi, a non-profit consultant, ran the very first conference dedicated to POC fundraisers and philanthropists called 'BAME Online'. Curating this virtual event was no small task. All their speakers were people of colour from across the charity and fundraising sector, and amongst the speakers they gave space for grassroots LGBTQ POC to speak about crowd-funding, what it means to distribute fundraising equity and what fundraising can learn from LGBTQ POC activists as well as more panels shaped by POC. When asked what made the conference such a success, Awojobi gave three reasons when speaking at bbcon 2020:

1. The speakers were diverse across all protected characteristics.

2. We reimagined what professionalism looked like.

3. We seized the opportunity to have a public conversation about systems change.

Awojobi had speakers from as many ethnic backgrounds

to showcase what BAME actually means, echoing that when organizations say BAME, there is often no Black staff. After a draft list of speakers Awojobi asked, 'Who is missing?' After finding trans, non-binary and East Asian people missing, they created more panels and curated space for their voices: 'Surely they're an essential part of the voluntary sector.' None of this was easy nor by accident, but putting together a diverse range of speakers is part of the job of event curators and project planners.

Conversations about whiteness

Good practice is conversations about whiteness held (quietly) by white people for white people.

— survey respondent

Whether these are dedicated 'privilege cafes', white allyship/solidarity networks or honest conversations between white friends, there needs to be spaces where white people are having discussions about their own experiences of whiteness amongst each other. Talk through your privilege checklist, unpack your invisible rucksacks together and challenge the racial microaggressons and stereotypes you play into. As mentioned in Section 1, these conversations should only be held with people who face the same privileges as you – people of colour don't need to know how your whiteness shows up and makes you feel, as people of colour experience this daily.

As someone who isn't white, I'm not privy to these spaces or networks existing, and as a person of colour I don't need to know when, where or how these conversations are happening either. This does not need to be a performance, be made public or take place for the benefit of people of colour. It is for the benefit of white people that these conversations are happening. It is the work of white people to ensure they exist. White supremacy needs to be dismantled for the benefit of everyone if everyone is truly concerned with racial equity and social justice.

Taking responsibility for racism and ableism

Transgender Europe (TGEU), an organization for the trans community in Europe since 2005, published an activity report, which they regularly publish, covering their work across 2016–2018. For the first time, they published an **anti-activity** report, offering a critical reflection of all the work across this period, specifically focusing on racism and ableism, talking not only about the successes but taking a 'power-critical look' at their activities and ways they realize they have left many people behind and failed their communities.

This worked because TGEU made public their failings, thus were publicly accountable for their failings. They clearly stated examples without identifiable information, stating, 'We reproduce racism/ableism when...' and then explaining how that example is racist and ableist. This may feel too late to those people their actions have hurt, which is acknowledged. It's also a witness to TGEU really seeing who makes up their trans communities. They concluded with commitments to undertake work to make radical and urgent changes, 'We acknowledge that resource distribution also needs to change... This includes an extensive reflection on the power Europe plays on the Global South, rethinking how we shape and handle our global projects, but also how our environmental practices affect other parts of the world' (TGEU, 2018, p.16) and what this means in practice, for example, 'Ensuring scholarships for our events which are only for Black and trans People of Colour, D/deaf and disabled trans people, for refugees and sex workers [and] having people from underrepresented groups in the selection process of scholarships, in hiring processes and in all decision-making processes' (TGEU, 2018, p.16).

TPOC-led youth work

Gendered Intelligence (GI), a national trans youth charity established in 2008, started a dedicated youth group for trans youth of colour in 2014 in London. Over the years it has changed names from BAME to Colours to TPOCalypse, all suggestions that have come directly from young people in order to name a group that reflects them. Flexibility and a youth-led approach is central to trans youth work practice at GI. There were some requests from young people wanting to join asking if they were 'allowed' to come as they're mixed race, and others were saying they don't feel BAME/POC enough to attend. The response to this was to write something explicit on the website to explain who the group is for and acknowledge the experience of feeling like you don't belong on top of navigating gender identity. It's important to affirm people in all parts of themselves to be in a space where they are safe to explore it more.

> The group is still dedicated to self-identifying trans young people of colour only. All workers and visitors will be trans or gender variant people of colour. We understand trans and

non-binary people of colour can experience additional barriers and stigma. TPOCalypse is designed as a safe space for young people of colour, with disabilities, with religious beliefs who are trans men, trans women, gender non-conforming or non-binary. We explicitly welcome and invite mixed-heritage people. It's okay if you don't feel black enough, or Asian enough, we welcome all young people of colour who are unsure or questioning their gender, or just looking to meet like-minded people. (Gendered Intelligence, 2021)

Ten ways to make your practice inclusive

1. **Be uncomfortable.** Think about what makes you uncomfortable and why. Name your fear, guilt, shame and be with it.

2. **Own your power.** Understand your privileges, influences and positions relating to TPOC communities on an individual and organizational level. Be responsible for your privilege and be accountable.

3. **Learn to apologize.** Part of allyship and solidarity work means making mistakes; that is how we all learn. Intention doesn't always matter. And when it happens: acknowledge, apologize and move through.

4. **Don't do nothing.** Inaction is still an action. Ask yourself: 'What can I do?'

5. **Talk about gender diversity and racial inequality.** Engage others in discussion, especially when we aren't there, and keep this conversation going.

6. **Keep listening.** Listen to Black youth and youth of colour, to trans and non-binary people of colour, to disabled, religious, working-class communities – share stories and amplify voices.

7. **Keep learning.** Inclusive practice is a commitment; bring it into all parts of your life. Unpack your invisible rucksack. Expand your reading lists, diversify your news sources and music and film consumption, and support TPOC businesses and causes.

8. **Include** TPOC **at every level.** Centre us, hire us, invest in us. Care about our communities and make space for us.

9. **Trust** TPOC. Let TPOC speak for TPOC experiences and communities, and believe us. We are experts by lived experience.

10. **Affirm us. Protect us. Love us.**

Section 7

Conclusion

The moment I spoke and wasn't heard, this book started writing itself. Trying to be seen was something I did alone, and for a long time I didn't expect anyone would join me, let alone ask me to speak up. As difficult as those first realizations were as The Only Trans Person/Person of Colour in the Room, I was still there in that room as a trans person of colour. I refused to not exist. I had the privilege of energy, time and safety to speak openly, so I spoke. Loud.

There was a turning point when I realized that speaking about all the ways in which I was oppressed was not helpful any more. It didn't help me, recounting the so-called tragedies of being a queer Muslim, the anticipated tales of the everyday harassment I get for being a trans person of colour. All in front of people who have more in common with the perpetrators than with those who have helped me. This didn't help them either; simply listening to my oppression does not make them a better person. We already know that oppression exists: events and blogs spotlighting marginalized people wouldn't exist if our experiences weren't already in the dark. I heard the same questions: 'How can you be trans and Muslim?', 'Have you experienced prejudice in your community?', 'What did your parents say?', which all affirm the notion that I can't be Muslim and trans, that I should expect to face prejudice within Muslim and LGBTQ communities and that my parents had something (negative) to say about all of it. I decided that I would change the way I spoke about myself. It's not enough to learn about oppression and disempowerment, about the barriers we face on institutional levels and micro levels. We need to learn about how we participate in oppression too. We need to learn about the powers we have that can disempower others. We need to learn about the ways we put up barriers on those institutional and micro levels. Because oppression does not exist without power. Inclusion doesn't happen without exclusion.

An audience can connect with a story and feel empathy for me having to go through hardship, but they often remain in their seats in their position as a spectator. It's only when we learn about our role in how we participate in oppression that we start to see ourselves as part of that story. We can position ourselves as the antagonist, protagonist or sidekick. It's not our story but we have a role. And our story must always be told.

This is what we do, trans people of colour: we continue to exist; we persist. We will continue to build spaces where we can do so safely and comfortably when other spaces turn us away. We will continue to model what it looks like when our community is cared for. Through protests, pandemics, uprisings and rulings, there is so much our communities have been through and can get through together. We build our homes with full hearts, not four walls, and we rewrite what it means to feel safe as trans people of colour through the internet and global unrest. We do this with patience; as trans people we learn to wait, to hold ourselves and each other whilst nothing changes. With power; as queer people, we make waves. When nothing changes, we resist, we protest. We know how to make change happen. With passion and compassion; as people of colour, we lead each other by the hand and we lead movements by the heart.

It's so not important when this particular story began, when I started writing it nor when you started reading it, because (un)fortunately this is still relevant. This tells me first that yes, there is so much more to say and so much more to do. Second, that this is something that you can come back to. Third, that we must keep coming back to this until it is no longer relevant. Hopefully by then our communities and spaces will be everyday, accessible, visible. They will be the whole movement and not just the peak, a spark, a protest or a death, but all the highs, lows, collaborating, recovering, healing and resting that happens outside of that. They will recognize that we need to be our own advocates sometimes and that we need community care and non-optical allyship other times. They will hear the voices of everyone, those silenced or spoken over. When all the community work we do is ultimately for younger generations, we need young people at every step of the way. They will say, 'nothing about us, without us', and we will listen.

Finally, this is not the complete guide on how to make your practice inclusive; this is really how to **start** making your practice inclusive. These pages in themselves will not be all-encompassing. Be curious about what's missing here and in your own practice or community. There are more questions to be asked, so start asking them of white people, cis people, allies and supporters. There are many more answers out there, so continue learning. Work with hospitality, prisons, therapists, teachers, schools, musicians, creatives, healthcare professionals – work with people across sectors, professions and regions, trans people of colour are everywhere. You will understand our communities, challenges and needs the more you get to know who we are. The wise words of the Queensland Aboriginal activist group (1970s[1]) remind us that our struggles are all connected, our guidance will take us forward and the benefits felt by one person will be felt by many: **'If you have come here to help me, you are wasting your time. But if you have come because your liberation is bound up with mine, then let us work together.'**

This is a process: working together and inclusivity is action after action, just like learning/unlearning/relearning. And at the heart of inclusivity is solidarity. Solidarity is, like the heart, a muscle; we need to move it, exercise it over and over. Over time we build strength and can sustain whole systems, but we need other muscles to support them and keep them going. Solidarity is not a yes or a no; it is not a tick box. Solidarity does not stay still; it is a movement and moves itself: it reacts, changes and connects to whatever a community needs. Solidarity asks, 'What can I do?' and does it. Then, it asks again.

This is a journey: wherever it begins, it begins with you, but doesn't have to end there. Perhaps someone else has joined you along the way. Maybe you're on more than one journey. The destination is not always important when exploring power and diversity – when we look ahead to the end, we're only

---

1   This quote was formed through a collective process with Aboriginal community organizers and leaders in Queensland going back to the 1970s, although it is not clear when exactly.

looking in one direction that feels comfortable or familiar for us. We can stay fixed in what we know, but there's a lot we miss and lose on the way. Where can you slow down to explore other directions? Where is your journey taking you? Is this still where you want to go? Make time and take time to explore your journey.

This is just the start.

References

Aboriginal Activists Group, Queensland (1970s). Attributing words. Accessed on 28/05/2021 at http://unnecessaryevils.blogspot.com/2008/11/attributing-words.html

Accapadi, M.M. (2007) When White Women Cry: How White Women's Tears Oppress Women of Colour. *The College Students Affair Journal 26*, 2, 208–215.

Adamson, S. (2020) People of colour vs. Black people. Accessed on 18/05/2021 at https://shadesofnoir.org.uk/people-of-colour-vs-black-people

Alabanza, T. (2017) *Before I Step Outside* [You Love Me]. UK: Travis Alabanza.

Alemoru, K. (2017) Gal-dem's bedroom: What's in a safe space? Accessed on 22/05/2021 at www.visithull.org/discover/gal-dems-bedroom-whats-safe-space-now

Al-Kadhi, A. (2019) *Life as a Unicorn*. London: 4th Estate.

Anzaldúa, G. (1998) To(o) Queer the Writer —*Loca, escritora y chicana.* In C. Trujillo (Ed.), *Living Chicana Theory* (p.264). San Antonio, TX: Third Woman Press.

Awojobi, M. (2020) Martha Awojobi: There are tangible ways charities can dismantle institutional racism. Accessed on 25/05/2021 at www.civilsociety.co.uk/voices/martha-awojobi-there-are-tangible-ways-charities-can-dismantle-institutional-racism.html

BARC (n.d.) Principled space. Accessed on 28/05/2021 at https://barcworkshop.org/resources/principled-space

Barker, M.-J. and Scheele, J. (2019) *Gender: A Graphic Guide.* London: Icon Books.

Bartholomew, E. (2019) 'We are all dealing with so much': Lady Phyll on why Black Pride UK is necessary ahead of Haggerston Park Festival. *Hackney Gazette.* Accessed on 28/05/2021 at www.hackneygazette.co.uk/news/lady-phyll-on-why-black-pride-uk-is-necessary-3628862

Bauder, D. (2020) AP says it will capitalize Black but not white. *Associated Press.* Accessed on 18/05/2021 at https://apnews.com/article/7e36c00c5af0436abc09e051261ffff1f

bbcon [bbcon 2020 Virtual] (2020) *Key steps to event curation success: Insights from the first ever BAME Conference* [Video]. Vimeo. Accessed on 28/05/2021 at https://vimeo.com/486171781/70ce49502e

Begum, T. (2020) This is how we can tackle anti-blackness in the South Asian community. Accessed on 22/05/2021 at https://i-d.vice.com/en_uk/article/ep4pmz/how-to-tackle-anti-black-racism-south-asian-community

Bergdorf, M. (2020) 'We show people what it is to be free.' Munroe Bergdorf is using her platform to celebrate Black trans lives. *Time.* Accessed on 25/05/2021 at https://time.com/collection-post/5896367/munroe-bergdorf-next-generation-leaders

Beyond the Binary (2016) Stonewall's trans BME consultation. Accessed on 06/05/2021 at http://web.archive.org/web/20200220171104/http://beyondthebinary.co.uk

Boccanto, A. (2020) Covid-19: race, class and the 'great equalizer' myth. Accessed on 25/05/2021 at https://charitysowhite.org/press/media-diversity-institute-race-class-and-the-great-equaliser-myth

Bornstein, K. (1994) *Gender Outlaw: On Men, Women, and the Rest of Us.* Oxfordshire: Routledge.

brown, a.m. (2017) *Emergent Strategy.* Chico, CA: AK Press.

Brown, B. (2006) Shame Resilience Theory: A Grounded Theory Study on Women and Shame. *Families in Society 87*, 1, 43–52.

Brown, B. (2012, March) Listening to shame [Video]. TED Conferences. www.ted.com/talks/brene_brown_listening_to_shame

Brown, B. (Host) (2020, July 1). Brené on shame and accountability [Audio podcast episode]. In *Unlocking Us with Brené Brown.* https://brenebrown.com/podcast/brene-on-shame-and-accountability

Bukari, R. (2020) Why the UK's first ever South Asian Heritage Month meant so much to me. Accessed on 03/07/2021 at https://gal-dem.com/first-south-asian-heritage-month-2020

Carbado, D. W. (2005) Privilege. In E. P. Johnson and M.G. Henderson (Eds.), *Black Queer Studies* (pp.190–212). Durham, NC: Duke University Press.

Cedar (2008) Cis privilege checklist: the cisgender/cissexual privilege checklist. Accessed on 18/05/2021 at https://takesupspace.wordpress.com/cis-privilege-checklist

Charity So White (2020) Racial injustice in the COVID-19 response. Accessed on 03/07/2021 at https://charitysowhite.org/covid19

Choudrey, S. (2016) Inclusivity: supporting BAME trans people. GIRES. Accessed on 23/05/2021 at www.gires.org.uk/wp-content/uploads/2016/02/BAME_Inclusivity.pdf

Counter-Terrorism and Security Act 2015, c.6. Accessed on 22/05/2021 at www.legislation.gov.uk/ukpga/2015/6/contents/enacted

CPT (2019) The cisgender privilege checklist. Accessed on 18/05/2021 at https://cpt.org/sites/default/files/2019-04/Undoing%20Heterosexism%20-%20The%20Cisgender%20Privilege%20Checklist.pdf

Crenshaw, K. (1989) Demarginalizing the Intersection of Race and Sex: A Black Feminist Critique of Antidiscrimination Doctrine, Feminist Theory and Antiracist Politics. *University of Chicago Legal Forum, 1989*, Article 8. Accessed on 22/05/2021 at https://chicagounbound.uchicago.edu/uclf/vol1989/iss1/8

Daikon (2018) Anti-Blackness in Asian communities. Accessed on 22/05/2021 at https://daikon.co.uk/blog/anti-blackness

Davis, S. (2017) Being a Queer and/or Trans Person of Colour in the UK: Psychology, Intersectionality and Subjectivity (Doctoral thesis, University of Brighton, Brighton, UK).

DiAngelo, Robin (2018) *White Fragility*. Boston: Beacon Press.

Diversity and Ability (n.d.) Resources. Accessed on 22/05/2021 at https://diversityandability.com/resources

Eddo-Lodge, R. (2018a) *Why I'm No Longer Talking to White People About Race*. London: Bloomsbury.

Eddo-Lodge, R. (Host) (2018b, 12 April) Political Blackness (No. 4) [Audio podcast episode]. In *About Race*. Accessed on 18/05/2021 at www.aboutracepodcast.com/4-political-blackness

Eddo-Lodge, R. (Host) (2018c, 17 May). The Big Question (No. 9) [Audio podcast episode]. In *About Race*. Accessed on 25/05/2021 at www.aboutracepodcast.com/9-the-big-question

Equality Act 2010, c.15. Accessed on 18/05/2021 at www.legislation.gov.uk/ukpga/2010/15/contents

Feder, S. (Director) (2020) *Disclosure* [Documentary]. Field of Vision, Bow and Arrow Entertainment and Level Forward.

Gendered Intelligence (2021) Trans youth work. Accessed on 28/05/2021 at https://genderedintelligence.co.uk/trans-youth/BAME

Grierson, J. (2021, March 17) Hundreds of Islamic groups boycott Prevent review over choice of chair. *The Guardian*. www.theguardian.com/uk-news/2021/mar/17/hundreds-islamic-groups-boycott-prevent-review-william-shawcross-protest

Gul, M. (2018) History of a marginalised community. Accessed on 17/05/2021 at www.dandc.eu/en/article/british-introduced-discrimination-transgender-persons-south-asia

Harper, M.C. (2020) If you want to be anti-racist, this non-optical allyship guide is required reading. Accessed on 25/05/2021 at www.vogue.co.uk/arts-and-lifestyle/article/non-optical-ally-guide

Hempstock, S. and Andry, S. (2017) Radical listening: A manifesto. *STRIKE! Magazine*. Accessed on 22/05/2021 at www.strike.coop/radical-listening-a-manifesto

Hislop, S. [Show Racism the Red Card] (2020, June 20) *Shaka Hislop on why 'All Lives Matter' is offensive* [Video]. YouTube. www.youtube.com/watch?v=DWo-JI7fmUU

Hord, L. and Medcalf, K. (2020a) Trans people's experience of the criminal justice system in England. TRANSforming Futures. Accessed on 22/05/2021 at www.transformingfuturespartnership.co.uk/healthcare

Hord, L. and Medcalf, K. (2020b) Trans people's experience of healthcare in England. TRANSforming Futures. Accessed on 22/05/2021 at www.transformingfuturespartnership.co.uk/healthcare

Hou, K. (2020) Munroe Bergdorf receives an apology from L'Oréal Paris. Accessed on 28/05/2021 at www.thecut.com/2020/06/munroe-bergdorf-receives-an-apology-from-loreal-paris-uk.html

Hubbard, E.A. (2017, July 28) Britain can't just reverse the homophobia it exported during the empire. *The Guardian*. Accessed on 17/05/2021 at www.theguardian.com/commentisfree/2017/jul/28/

britain-reverse-homophobia-empire-criminlisation-homosexuality-colonies

Hudson, P.J. (2014) Canada and the Question of Black Geographies: An Interview with Katherine McKittrick. *The CLR James Journal.*

Human Rights Act 1998, c.42. Accessed on 18/05/2021 at www.legislation.gov.uk/ukpga/1998/42/schedule/1/part/I/chapter/9

Iantaffi, A. and Barker, M.-J. (2018) *How to Understand Your Gender.* London: Jessica Kingsley Publishers.

Incite! (n.d.) Community accountability. Accessed on 25/05/2021 at https://incite-national.org/community-accountability

Inclusive Mosque Initiative (2016) Statement of intent. Accessed on 28/05/2021 at https://inclusivemosque.org/statement-of-intent

Intersex Equality Rights UK (n.d.) Accessed on 03/07/2021 at www.consortium.lgbt/member-directory/intersex-equality-rights-uk

Iqbal, N. (2019, February 16) Academic Robin DiAngelo: 'We have to stop thinking about racism as someone who says the N-word'. *The Guardian.* Accessed on 18/05/2021 at www.theguardian.com/world/2019/feb/16/white-fragility-racism-interview-robin-diangelo

Jeraj, S. (2014) Sharing the experience of being black and minority ethnic and trans. Race Equality Foundation. Accessed on 03/07/2021 at http://ref.hybiscas.com/wp-content/uploads/Event%20report%20-%20Sharing%20the%20experience%20of%20being%20black%20and%20minority%20ethnic%20and%20trans%20final.pdf

Joseph, C. (2020) Bookmark this: the BAME acronym is often reductive and lazy. Accessed on 14/09/2021 at https://gal-dem.com/bookmark-this-are-acronyms-like-bame-a-nonsense

Juang, M.R. (2006) Transgendering the Politics of Recognition. In S. Stryker and S. Whittle (Eds.), *The Transgender Studies Reader* (pp.706–719). New York: Routledge.

Justice Funders (2020) Dismantling white supremacy & anti-Blackness in philanthropy. Accessed on 25/05/2021 at https://medium.com/justice-funders/dismantling-white-supremacy-anti-blackness-in-philanthropy-7256abbbb3c4

Kattari, S.K., Whitfield, D.L., De Chants, J. and Alvarez, A.R.G. (2016) Barriers to health faced by transgender and non-binary black and minority ethnic people: Better Health Briefing Paper 41. Race Equality Foundation. Accessed on 18/05/2021 at https://raceequalityfoundation.org.uk/wp-content/uploads/2018/02/Better-Health-41-Trans-NB-final.pdf

Kaur, R. (2020) Language barriers: how our words obscure bias and discrimination. Accessed on 18/05/2021 https://charitysowhite.org/blog/language-barriers-how-our-words-obscure-bias-and-discrimination

Kendi, I.X. (2019) *How to Be an Antiracist*. London: Random House.

Kim, M. (2020) 30+ ways Asians perpetuate anti-Black racism everyday. Accessed on 22/05/2021 at https://medium.com/awaken-blog/30-ways-asians-perpetuate-anti-black-racism-everyday-32886c9b3075

Koyama, E. (2006) Whose Feminism Is It Anyway? The Unspoken Racism of the Trans Inclusion Debate. In S. Stryker and S. Whittle (Eds.), *The Transgender Studies Reader* (pp.698–705). New York: Routledge.

Kuchenga, (2020) Hirschfeld's follies. Accessed on 25/05/2021 at http://adventuresintimeandgender.org/wormholes/erasure

LanguageLine (n.d.) Accessed on 25/05/2021 at www.languageline.com/uk

Lester, CN (2011) 'No cis guys' – no thank you. Accessed on 22/05/2021 at https://cnlester.wordpress.com/2011/11/28/no-cis-guys-no-thank-you

Lewis, T. (2021) 2021 working definition of ableism. Accessed on 22/05/2021 at www.talilalewis.com/blog/january-2021-working-definition-of-ableism

List of minor secular observances (2021, May 24) In *Wikipedia*. Accessed on 25/05/2021 at https://en.wikipedia.org/wiki/List_of_minor_secular_observances

List of multinational festivals and holidays (2021, May 25) In *Wikipedia*. Accessed on 25/05/2021 at https://en.wikipedia.org/wiki/List_of_multinational_festivals_and_holidays

London Bi Pandas (n.d.) Alternatives to calling the police. Accessed on 22/05/2021 at www.londonbipandas.com/blog/alternatives-to-calling-the-police

Lorde, A. (1982) Learning from the 60s. Accessed on 18/05/2021 at www.blackpast.org/african-american-history/1982-audre-lorde-learning-60s

Marshall, L. (2016) LGBTQ+ nightlife spaces in London. Accessed on 28/05/2021 at www.ucl.ac.uk/urban-lab/research/research-projects/LGBTQ-nightlife-spaces-london

McIntosh, P. (1988) White Privilege and Male Privilege: A Personal Account of Coming to See Correspondences through Work in Women's Studies. Working Paper 189.

McIntosh, P. (1989) White Privilege: Unpacking the Invisible Knapsack. Accessed on 22/09/2021 at https://nationalseedproject.org/Key-SEED-Texts/white-privilege-unpacking-the-invisible-knapsack

Microsoft (n.d.) Office accessibility centre – resources for people with disabilities. Accessed on 22/05/2021 at https://support.microsoft.com/en-us/topic/office-accessibility-center-resources-for-people-with-disabilities-ecabofcf-d143-4fe8-a2ff-6cd596bddc6d?ui=en-us&rs=en-gb&ad=gb

Mingus, M. (2011) Access intimacy: the missing link. Accessed on 22/05/2021 at https://leavingevidence.wordpress.com/2011/05/05/access-intimacy-the-missing-link

Mirza, A. (2020) Queeries: how can I, as a non-black person of colour, help dismantle anti-blackness? Accessed on 22/05/2021 at https://gal-dem.com/queeries-how-can-i-as-a-non-black-person-of-colour-help-dismantle-anti-blackness

Mitchell, H. (2021) Meet Dr Ronx Ikharia, the inspiring trans, non-binary trailblazer and activist you need to know about. Accessed on 25/05/2021 at www.pinknews.co.uk/2021/01/07/dr-ronx-ikharia-trans-non-binary

Moses, G. (2019) 7 ways to make your social justice space accessible to disabled people. Accessed on 03/07/2021 at https://thebodyisnotanapology.com/magazine/7-ways-to-make-your-social-justice-space-accessible-to-disabled-people

Munir, M. (2020) Interview with campaign bootcamp. Accessed on 22/05/2021 at https://campaignbootcamp.org/wp-content/uploads/2020/05/Bootcamp-talks-to...Maria_-Transcript-1-3.pdf

Obear, K. (2021) ...But I'm not racist, am I? Accessed on 22/05/2021 at https://drkathyobear.com/racequiz

Office for National Statistics (n.d.) Accessed on 25/05/2021 at www.ons.gov.uk

OOI (n.d.) OOI Intersex Network. Accessed on 03/07/2021 at https://oiiinternational.com

OOI-UK (n.d.) Organisation Intersex International in the United Kingdom. Accessed on 03/07/2021 at https://oiiuk.org

Public Order Act 1986, c.64. Accessed on18/05/2021 at www.legislation.gov.uk/ukpga/1986/64/section/4

Qasim, W. (2016) Being a black, British, queer, non-binary Muslim isn't a contradiction. *The Guardian.* www.theguardian.com/commentisfree/2016/jun/20/black-british-queer-non-binary-muslim-isnt-contradiction

Quah, M. (2020) How the British Empire globalised transphobia. Accessed on 17/05/2021 at https://redactionpolitics.com/2020/09/04/how-the-british-empire-globalised-transphobia

Queer Spaces Network (2018) A Vision for Queer Cultural Spaces in London. In B. Campkin, L. Marshall and R. Ross (Eds.) *Urban Pamphleteer #7: LGBTQ+ Night-Time Spaces, Past, Present and Future.* London: Urban Pamphleteer.

Rage, R. (2020) Access intimacy and institutional ableism: Raju Rage on the problem with 'inclusion'. Accessed on 22/05/2021 at https://disabilityarts. online/magazine/opinion/access-intimacy-and-institutional-ableism-raju-rage-on-the-problem-with-inclusion

Ralph, N. (2020) When I'm not on twitter I spend my life training activists, campaigners and change-makers on how to make effective, strategic and regenerative social change. In movement theory there is a concept of a 'movement lifecycle' which I think is really important for ppl to know about rn [Tweet]. Accessed on 28/05/2021 at https://twitter.com/ NMRLPH/status/1273260325308153857

Raza-Sheikh, Z. (2020) Tanya Compas is a youth worker and activist spreading LGBTQ+ love through humanity and humility. *Gay Times.* Accessed on 22/05/2021 at www.gaytimes.co.uk/amplify/tanya-compas-interview

Ridwan, R. (2020) What happened when seven trans people of colour were given space to chat shit. Accessed on 22/05/2021 at https://gal-dem.com/ what-happened-when-seven-trans-people-of-colour-were-given-space-to-chat-shit

Saad, L. (2018) *Me and White Supremacy.* London: Quercus.

Seeds for Change (n.d.) Venues and accessibility. Accessed on 22/05/2021 at www.seedsforchange.org.uk/access

Serano, J. (2007) *Whipping Girl.* New York: Seal Press.

Serano, J. (2013) FAAB-mentality. Accessed on 22/05/2021 at http://juliaserano. blogspot.com/2013/03/faab-mentality.html

Shahid, N. (2020) The pandemic is trauma for disabled people. Accessed on 22/05/2021 at www.autostraddle.com/the-pandemic-is-trauma-for-trans-disabled-people

Shelley, B. (2016) 'Everyone but cis men': creating better safe spaces for LGBT people. Accessed on 22/05/2021 at https://the-toast.net/2016/04/18/ everyone-but-cis-men-creating-better-safe-spaces-for-lgbt-people

Shulevitz, J. (2015, March 15) In college and hiding from scary ideas. *New York Times.* Accessed on 22/05/2021 at www.nytimes.com/2015/03/22/opinion/ sunday/judith-shulevitz-hiding-from-scary-ideas.html

Sin, V. (2018) Drag's Humour Should Be at the Expense of Gender, Not Women. In B. Campkin, L. Marshall and R. Ross (Eds.) *Urban Pamphleteer #7: LGBTQ+ Night-Time Spaces, Past, Present and Future.* London: Urban Pamphleteer.

Singh, S.R. (2015) Recipes and Rites. In A. S. Duttchoudhury and R. Hartman (Eds.), *Moving Truth(s): Queer and Transgender Desi Writings on Family* (pp.156–171). Seattle: Flying Chickadee.

Sisters Uncut (2018) Safer spaces policy. Accessed on 22/05/2021 at www.sistersuncut.org/saferspaces

Slater, J. and Jones, C. (2020) The toilet debate: Stalling trans possibilities and defending 'women's protected spaces'. *The Sociological Review, 68,* 4, 834–851.

Snoussi, D. and Mompelat, L. (2019) 'We are ghosts': race, class and institutional prejudice. The Runnymede Trust and The Centre for Labour and Social Studies. Accessed on 25/05/2021 at www.runnymedetrust.org/uploads/publications/We%20Are%20Ghosts.pdf

Soni, A. (2020) Five things to share on Intersex Awareness Day. Accessed on 22/-5/2021 at www.ukblackpride.org.uk/blog/2020/10/26/five-things-to-share-on-intersex-awareness-day

South Asians for Black Lives (2020) Accessed on 22/05/2021 at www.malikah.org/south-asians-for-black-lives

Sprout Distro (2017) 12 things to do instead of calling the cops. Accessed on 22/05/2021 at https://ia800800.us.archive.org/1/items/12ThingsToDoInsteadOfCallingTheCops/12things-screen.pdf

Stephens, A. (2020, May 28). Black trans men face constant threat of police violence. *The Advocate.* Accessed on 22/05/2021 at www.advocate.com/commentary/2020/5/28/black-trans-men-face-constant-threat-police-violence

Stonewall (2018) Stonewall's attendance at Pride events in 2018. Accessed on 28/05/2021 at www.stonewall.org.uk/node/63216

Strossen, N. (2018) *HATE: Why We Should Resist It with Free Speech, Not Censorship.* Oxford: Oxford University Press.

Sue, D.W., Capodilupo, C.M., Torino, G.C., Bucceri, J.M., Holder, A.M.B., Nadal, K. L., and Esquilin, M. (2007) Racial Microaggressions in Everyday Life: Implications for Clinical Practice. *American Psychologist, 62,* 4, 271–286.

The British Library (Host) (2021, January 19) Trans through time [Audio podcast episode]. In Unfinished Business. Accessed on 18/05/2021 at https://podcastc41509.podigee.io/8-trans-through-time

The Chartered Institute of Fundraising (2021) Recruitment guides. Accessed on 25/05/2021 at https://ciof.org.uk/about-us/what-we-re-doing/equality,-diversity-and-inclusion/recruitment-guides-(1)

The Movement Lab (2016) Movement cycles in the struggle for Black lives. Accessed on 28/05/2021 at https://movementnetlab.org/movement-cycles-in-the-struggle-for-black-lives

The National LGB&T Partnership (n.d.) Trans health factsheet on BAME people. Accessed on 03/07/2021 at https://nationallgbtpartnershipdotorg.files.wordpress.com/2015/02/np-trans-health-factsheet-bame.pdf

The Runnymede Trust and The Centre for Labour and Social Sciences (2019) Race and class messaging toolkits. Accessed on 09/05/2021 at www.runnymedetrust.org/projects-and-publications/employment-3/we-are-ghosts-race-class-and-institutional-prejudice.html

The Unitarian Universalist Association (n.d.) Alternatives to calling the police. Safe Congregations Handbook. Accessed on 22/05/2021 at www.uua.org/safe/handbook/alternatives-calling-police

The Unmistakeables (n.d.) Despora photo collection. Accessed on 25/05/2021 at www.theunmistakables.com/despora

TGEU (2018) Activity report: Transgender Europe's activities from June 2016 until June 2018. Accessed on 28/05/2021 at https://tgeu.org/activity-report-2016-2018

Thomas, L. [@glowmaven] (2018, May 1) There are people who are truly energized and moved to work to improve the lives of marginalized people. Accessed on 25/05/2021 at www.instagram.com/p/BiPDZkbFJFY

Towle, E.B. and Morgan, L.M. (2006) Romancing the Transgender Native: Rethinking the Use of the 'Third Gender' Concept. In S. Stryker and S. Whittle (Eds.), *The Transgender Studies Reader* (pp.666–684). New York: Routledge.

Truitt, J. (2012) Enough with 'I date women and trans men.' Accessed on 22/05/2021 at http://feministing.com/2012/06/28/enough-with-i-date-women-and-trans-men

Twilight People (2017a) Anjeli: Hinduism, unity and making a difference. Accessed on 22/05/2021 at www.twilightpeople.com/anjeli-hinduism-unity-making-difference

Twilight People (2017b) CJ: I have a gender. Accessed on 22/05/2021 at www. twilightpeople.com/cj-i-gender

Unison (2016) Responding to the 'Prevent Duty'. Accessed on 03/07/2021 at www.unison.org.uk/content/uploads/2016/10/Prevent-Duty.pdf

Uwujaren, J. (2013) *The difference between cultural exchange and cultural appropriation.* Accessed on 22/05/2021 at https://everydayfeminism.com/ 2013/09/cultural-exchange-and-cultural-appropriation

Valerio, N. (2019) This viral Facebook post urges people to rethink self-care. Accessed on 25/05/2021 at www.flare.com/identity/self-care-new-zealand-muslim-attack

Van Loon, K. (2012) Calling for an International Non-Binary Gender Day. Accessed on 28/05/2021 at https://femmesblackmarket.wordpress. com/2012/03/08/calling-for-an-international-non-binary-gender-day

White, F. [Adventures in Gender and Time Podcast] (2020, October 26) *Dr Francis Ray White – not another talk about toilets* [Video]. YouTube. www. youtube.com/watch?v=wzse3JjiaAM

Williams, C. (2020) The UK is complicit in antiblack racism – and has a responsibility to fight it. Accessed on 22/05/2021 at https://fortune. com/2020/06/17/black-systemic-racism-uk-ftse

Wilks-Harper, E. (2016) There is a fine line between tokenism and diversity. Accessed on 25/05/2021 at https://gal-dem.com/fine-line-tokenism-diversity-media/

Yes Magazine (2020) Let's talk about anti-Blackness. Accessed on 22/05/2021 at www.yesmagazine.org/education/2020/04/07/lets-talk-about-anti-blackness

Zachiyah, S. (2019) Brotherhood: a conversation on what it means to be trans men of colour in the UK. *Gay Times.* Accessed on 09/05/2021 at www. gaytimes.co.uk/life/brotherhood-a-conversation-on-what-it-means-to-be-trans-men-of-colour-in-the-uk-amplify-by-gay-times

Zoom (n.d.) Accessibility features. Accessed on 22/05/2021 at https://zoom. us/accessibility

Index